Becoming Lady

Enjoy! Love,

Jeanne
and
Lady

Enjoy! Love,

Jeanne
and
Lady

Becoming Lady

~

A Rescued Golden's Journey
from Lonely to Loved

Lady and Jeanne Maxon

TWO HARBORS PRESS
MINNEAPOLIS, MN

www.TwoHarborsPress.com

Copyright © 2015 by Jeanne Maxon

Two Harbors Press
322 First Avenue N, 5th floor
Minneapolis, MN 55401
612.455.2293
www.TwoHarborsPress.com

ISBN-13: 978-1-63413-516-0
LCCN: 2015906548

Distributed by Itasca Books

Book Design by B. Cook

Printed in the United States of America

Dedication

This book is dedicated to every kind soul whose love
nurtures a rescued dog.

.

Contents

Acknowledgments

Our family and friends

Their love, support, and enthusiasm kept us focused, and their humor kept us grounded. Their generous advance book orders give us hope. Forever thanks to our sister, Janet, who was with us every peck of the keyboard.

Bode Maxon

Our rock—who embodies all that is irresistible in the golden retriever breed. With Buddha-like patience, Bode selflessly shared his Jeanne, his home, and a specified portion of his king-size bed to help Lady be all she can be.

Diane Alexander

A lover of goldens, she donated her amazing professional photography skills to help us tell Lady's story. Front and back cover photos are her work.

Dory Mayo

Her belief in this book inspired us, and her flawless care for its editing awed us. More importantly, she became our friend in the process of helping make our book professional.

Rick Kaplan

The president and founder of Canine Angels, Inc., Rick orchestrated Lady's rescue and consulted with us tirelessly on her training. As she attests in one diary entry, "I'd be lost if not for you."

Preface

My name is Jeanne.

Memories of the misty March morning when I first saw Lady are permanently etched on my soul. I had driven to a house an hour away to meet her. My mission was to assess whether I could foster and help train her as a service dog for a disabled veteran. Her owner wanted to donate Lady to the group I volunteer with—Canine Angels—a nonprofit that trains rescued dogs to serve those who gave so much to our nation.

Lady was a two-year-old golden retriever who had spent all of her impressionable young life in a chain-link pen with practically no personal attention or human companionship. When at first I walked quietly into her view, she crouched nervously and stared blankly. I wondered if there was anyone home behind those eyes. Then her tail began a slow-motion swish, and she inched toward me on her belly. Her instincts were telling her to give me a chance. Mine were too.

I could barely stand to leave her waiting in her pen while I reorganized my life to foster and train a new member of our pack. Nearly a month later, I took Lady home. My eyes fill up with tears when I recall the stunning ease with which she chose to trust me with her life. She changed us both forever, giving as much as she got—every day of our partnership.

Lady wrote this book to bring her heartwarming journey to others who might laugh and learn from it. She also strives to show how rescued dogs can be all that they can be, and more—that is, when they have someone to love and guide *them*.

This is Lady's story.

Introduction

My name is Lady.

If you had seen me on the day I was rescued, you would say that my name didn't fit. My golden retriever coat was filthy, matted, and rain soaked from living outside.

But now I am transformed. I've attended fund-raising galas dressed to the nines in my pink Dollar Store bandanna. I've learned a touch of French and countless obedience commands in English. I've ridden on speedboats and golf carts, taken a challenging therapy dog test, and made a whole lot of people smile. And I've learned what it's like to be adored.

My life changed forever when Jeanne chose to foster and train me. The switch from sleeping fitfully on cement to stretching out on the cloud of a king-size bed was the first of many luxuries to come. So thrilled was I with life in my new indoor home that I took pen to paw and kept a daily journal, which I called the *Lady Grams* (like telegrams). Every day for more than two months I wrote an entry describing my training and many of the funny, heartwarming happenings along the way.

Together, Jeanne and I learned what being a foster team is all about. It's a lot of work, a lot of laughter, a lot of joyful tears, a few not-so-happy tears, and an immeasurable source of pride.

Even though I'm simply a dog, Jeanne says that I greeted each day of this journey with the courage of a lion. I am so proud.

This is my story, *Becoming Lady*.

Belly-Crawling into the Future

Dear Diary,

Day 1. Up to now and for nearly two long years in my pen, every day has been the same. Not today. As I lie licking the toes of my right hind foot, I hear an unfamiliar footfall. Through the chain-link I see a stranger approaching my pen, holding a leash and a collar. She speaks softly in a voice that I like. In an instant, I sense I can trust her and lower my guard. Even though I am scared, a tentative wag of welcome betrays my soft heart, and I belly-crawl toward the gate . . .

Love,

Lady

My Journey to Service Begins

Dear Diary,

Day 2. The water bowls are too small here. In my old outdoor pen I used to jump into a thirty-gallon tub for a drink. Other than that, my first full day of foster life in a real house has been fun, and I suspect I'll like being an indoor dog.

All the new things I've been exposed to since I crept into the car yesterday morning threatened to send me into sensory overload. My first long ride, the fifty-minute trip home, had gone well, and I was eager to begin life with my new pack: Jeanne, me, and Bode—a fellow golden retriever.

When we got home, I was treated to a soothing, warm indoor shower to wash away two years of dirt caked on my coat. It felt good. Then I took a long walk with Jeanne and Bode to survey the new neighborhood. I saw other dogs and people walking around here, but we won't visit them until we're sure we all have a positive attitude toward one another. Not sure what that is, but Jeanne seems to think it wise. I had never before heard traffic up close, yet the cars and trucks going by didn't bother me. They have golf carts here, and I'm intrigued. I think I would like to have one.

I love the floors in Jeanne's kitchen, laundry room, and half-bath. They're nice and cool for

Lady chooses her "just right" spot.

3

my naps, which I've taken three of so far—one in each spot, just like Goldilocks. So far, my "just right" spot is on the half-bath's tile floor with my head sticking through the doorway.

When I'm not napping, I follow Jeanne everywhere, because you simply never know whether she might escape out a door I hadn't noticed. She sure travels a lot of miles in a day. I think I've already lost a pound or two.

We noticed that I needed my nails trimmed, but there's only so much a lady should be asked to endure on Day 2. Jeanne says it will just have to wait.

I haven't minded the noise of the washer or dryer, and the dishwasher is okay. I'm told the vacuum might be an issue, but that's also for another day.

One thing that really doesn't appeal to me is eliminating on leash. Over the last two years, I had grown quite accustomed to going at will in the privacy of my outdoor pen. Today I held out as long as I could but then finally surrendered. I figured that Jeanne wasn't going to give up on this point, and we could be out there walking for days.

As another test, I was confined behind a gate in the laundry room, alone for thirty minutes while Jeanne and Bode went for a bike ride. I enjoyed a snooze in the quiet, and they woke me when they got back.

Tonight will see yet another "first" when I sleep in my carpeted kennel in the master bedroom. (I had been sequestered in the laundry room for night one.) Since I'm told that tomorrow we start initial training, whatever that is, I hope to get a good night's rest. Jeanne seems to think it will be fun, so I just want to be ready.

I am so happy and proud to be the new member of this pack.

Love and licks,

Lady

Fitting into the Pack

Dear Diary,

Day 3. Just when I thought I'd found a big enough water bowl, Jeanne ran in and slammed down the lid. So then I found a second one. She shut that lid, too. Guess I'll just have to stick with the little bowl on my rug in the laundry room. Sigh . . .

At nine thirty last night all three of us fell asleep on the human bed, and when we woke up at one thirty it was too late to entice me into my kennel. Not to worry, I could get to love that big, soft bed. We went back to sleep till five a.m., then out for me and Bode to "wee wee."

Since I used to be fed only at suppertime, I was confused when served breakfast. I ate none of the first offering and only half of the second. I didn't mind that Bode finished the leftovers, although Jeanne wasn't too happy because he's on a special diet. The food is good here, so it won't take long for me to look forward to wolfing down two meals a day.

Jeanne talks a lot. Her voice is soft and reassuring, but human talk is new to me. While I don't yet have Bode's extensive vocabulary, I'm sure I'll catch up in no time.

We had two unplanned visits this evening. First I met Rayne, the next-door neighbors' two-year-old daughter. She approached me with an outstretched hand which, of course, I licked. Then she told me, "You're a nice puppy." I instantly liked her, but our visit was understandably brief and controlled. Later, a different neighbor, Kona the yellow lab, escaped his master and ran over to me. I was guarded but not aggressive. Someday we'll become friends.

Bode and I are still negotiating our relationship. He's accommodating, yet he doesn't like to play with me. I'm told that could change as he adjusts to me as a new pack member.

Love, and learning *not* to lick,

Lady

Just Remember I'm a Dog

Dear Diary,

Day 4. I can't say we weren't warned, but it happened anyhow. During our morning walk we came across a man strolling along with his six-pound Chinese crested. The little bully barked, snarled, and strained at her leash in a determined attempt to attack me. I was ready to retaliate with equally ugly behavior, so Jeanne quickly turned us away from the fracas and headed home. Thoroughly upset and furious, I slipped my collar, tore after the little nuisance, and launched my entire seventy-one pounds at her. Defying a barrage of human shouting, I managed to get in one glancing nip. Then Jeanne literally tackled me and got my collar back on. Luckily, thanks to our pack leaders, no physical damage was done.

We're home now, and I'm dozing under Jeanne's computer chair. I can sense her looking into my sweet, beautiful face and thinking about my behavior. Then, with resignation, she tells herself that I am a dog. We were reminded of that in short order this morning.

On a more positive note, I was introduced to Catcher today. She's the uber-alpha Chesapeake Bay retriever girl-next-door who used to spend lots of time at my house. Her visits have been curtailed since my arrival to make my adjustment easier. This afternoon Catcher and I met on neutral turf and took a short, leashed walk with our humans. We negotiated a thirty-second mutual sniff punctuated by intense tail wagging. Apparently humans consider this a huge success, so Catcher and I agreed that it was cool. We'll meet again and again as they gradually extend our time together. I hope we can relax and become best buds one step at a time.

The highlight of my day was a car ride to the bank and the drugstore. Did you know that these places have windows designated purely for giving out cookies to dogs? Awesome!

Love,

Lady

Anxiety in the Air

Dear Diary,

Day 5. Each day I wake up happy—wiggling, snorting, stretching, rolling around, kicking the air, and snuggling into my packmates. Jeanne laughs. Bode tolerates me with endearing stoicism.

I'm just starting my fourth day of indoor living with no elimination mistakes. Although Jeanne tells me I'm amazing, I believe that my success is due to her unflagging efforts to take me outside on a strict schedule. This works for me, and for most dogs as well.

I could smell anxiety in the air in our house today. I heard Jeanne constantly muttering about tomorrow—April fifteenth—something called "taxes." I don't know what these words mean, but I could sense they were causing her stress. Resting my head on Jeanne's leg didn't even help. In fact, I got introduced to the command, "Away." So Bode and I laid low and tried to become invisible. This tax thing makes me glad I'm a dog.

Fast-forward to a few hours later: "tax" seems to have gone away. We celebrated by teaching me to run alongside the bike while Jeanne pedals. For now we're restricted to our cul-de-sac (yup, learning French, too), but gradually we'll venture farther out into the world. It was great exercise for me, as I

Lady learns to keep a safe distance from the bike while jogging.

9

pranced proudly up and down our street with my beautiful feathered coat fanning out behind me.

Love,
Lady

Oops, I'm in the Doghouse

Dear Diary,

Day 6 found me in the proverbial doghouse. If there had been a real one here, I would've been looking out from inside. Today I stood accused of a mortal sin.

I attacked Bode. Yes, the darling of the disabled, the hero of second-grade readers, the star of the neighborhood—and more's the shame, Jeanne's Number One Being on the Planet. I couldn't have picked a better (or is it worse?) dog to go after.

It wasn't personal. He tried to eat my supper. End of conversation.

No vet bills ensued. No blood was spilled. But admittedly, it was not a pretty sight. In my own defense, for the last two years and up until five days ago, any disputes with my former penmate were settled by . . . well, we duked it out. It's not as though I simply could have asked Bode to kindly return my dinner. Anyhow, a few minutes later we were friends again.

Jeanne figured that I have a touch of fear aggression on top of a little territorial aggression. So, on comes my leash whenever I eat. And she stands and watches until both of us are finished eating. If I even glance in Bode's direction, I get a sharp, fast leash correction accompanied by the "leave it" command. Her plan, as I understand it, is to have Bode and me eating calmly beside one another within a week. I'll try hard because that's my nature. I do love to please.

Love,
Lady

And on the *Seventh* Day . . .

Dear Diary,

Day 7. Haven't I heard some saying about "on the *seventh* day they rested?" Not in this three-pack.

Today began with our usual "wee wee" walk, then the new breakfast ritual in which Bode and I are learning to eat side-by-side without encroaching, growling, or worse. I made good progress toward this challenge, and I got a C+ on the week one report card.

Next, I ran a mile and a half next to the bike, earning an A-. The standard requires me to keep the same distance from the bike, regardless of speed. Most important, I *must* ignore all distractions, such as squirrels, cars, rabbits, birds, and non-pack people and dogs. It is essential to obey the command, "Leave it."

After biking, we played beauty parlor. Teeth brushing got me an easy B because I love that beef toothpaste. Ear cleaning got me an A, and coat brushing an A-. Nail filing with the Dremel was my downfall. I earned a D on this task due to my fear of the noise. Well, that beats an F anyhow. So far all I can tolerate is to have the Dremel near my feet but not turned on. Hope to clock some improvement by next week.

Throughout all this, we discovered that I love cheese, and Jeanne capitalizes on it every time I successfully achieve a training task. What I won't do for the tiniest cube of mozzarella!

Excitement ran rampant here today because, all by myself, I worked out a signal to ask to go out to eliminate. I go to the front door and stand patiently with my head turned into the room. This requires that Jeanne pay attention to my whereabouts whenever I'm not confined. Since I'm still following her most everywhere, that's easy enough.

Rumor in the pack has it that we get the rest of Sunday off. This certainly has been the most active and exciting week of my life. Will I *ever* be glad to spend the afternoon resting on that cool tile floor.

Love,
Lady

Girls Club

Dear Diary,

Day 8. Of all the new experiences I've had in just one week, one of the best was meeting Rayne, the almost-three-year-old who lives next door. Instabond!

She loves me because my coat is soft and our hair is the same color—and also because I nuzzle her gently, licking her hands, not her face.

I love *her* because I'm a golden. At eye level, she's just the right size. Staring at kneecaps all day gets old. Sometimes there's a crumb or a spill on her jersey that smells simply divine. Rayne always speaks her mind. Last night she said, "Lady, you have eye boogies." A girl needs to know these things.

Love,
Lady

Lady and Rayne become fast friends.

The Things That Matter

Dear Diary,

Day 9. I could just hug myself when I think about all that I've learned in what seemed like a very long week! Imagine—living *inside* a house that's actually a home teeming with a myriad assortment of sights, smells, and sounds. This morning Jeanne told me that she was "justifiably proud" of my bravery as I loaded up into a strange car to begin a risky new adventure with someone I had sniffed only twice. She marveled at the courage I showed as I stepped into an unfamiliar house, explored every corner, checked out the contents, and leaped onto a bed to lie down with a dog and a human I barely knew.

Up to now, I've met at least ten dogs and thirty or so people, easily double what I encountered in the two years spent in my old pen. Today I even joined a kayak club. Boo-yah! And I was applauded royally for not jumping into the water to chase the paddlers down the Waccamaw River! Believe me when I tell you that I was sorely tempted.

One last thing about today. Jeanne asked me a really dumb question. (I mean, we are blondes, but puh-leese!) Why is it, she said, that the elapsed time for me to learn the word "cheese," including knowing that it's kept in the fridge, was about one minute, yet the elapsed time for learning the command "down" is now up around a thousand minutes and counting. Well, duh. Isn't it all about motivation? I did know the word "down" right away. But I figure it'll take quite a few morsels of "cheese" to make it stick.

I'm beginning to grasp what's important to Jeanne and, she reminds me, what will be important to the service member who eventually will adopt me. But I don't like to talk about that too much . . .

Love,

Lady

Boot Camp Life

Dear Diary,

Day 10. When I am placed with my adopting service member, we'll have in common at least one fundamental experience: each of us will have been to boot camp. Although mine was not on a military installation, have no doubt that I, too, had a drill sergeant (Jeanne) and that the training was intense, challenging, and exhausting.

Just like barracks life, there is no privacy for any member of my pack; we all bunk together. You are told what and when to eat, and it had better be eaten with gusto. If you come up for air, the food is gone. Either Bode has eaten it, or Jeanne has removed it because (she accuses) I was grazing.

Good manners and learning to get along with others are crucial aspects of the training in both kinds of boot camp. Sometimes it seems that in one day you can get orders enough to last a lifetime. Trainees are required to dress alike. My uniform is a plain collar and leash, clearly not a fashion statement. But I am told that once I master certain skills, I will be awarded a special vest to wear in public that will identify the vital job entrusted to me.

The "at ease" command is a favorite.

Today I learned a command that's popular with service members and service dogs alike. It's my personal favorite, called "at ease."

Love,

Lady

Adventures at Bark Park

Dear Diary,

Day 11. Today's challenge was Bark Park. I'd been having a little dog-ag-gression issue, so Jeanne thought we should do some exercises to get past it. Bode and I loaded up into Lulu (our Subaru Outback), and off we sped with all manner of leashes, collars, balls, and treats at the ready.

We arrived at the park, which turned out to be crowded with people and dogs. So Jeanne drove right past it, wondering if perhaps this adventure might be more than I could tolerate. Then we decided to "cowboy up" and try. As I watched from Lulu, Jeanne and Bode entered the large-dog enclosure first and greeted everyone. Jeanne asked if they would mind if she brought in a poten-tially dog-aggressive golden on leash and under her control. One lady suggest-ed that she bring me into the small-dog section first, since it was empty.

That worked out quite well. I got the lay of the land and also could see, smell, and hear the big guys in the adjacent area. Once I was calm, we moved into the large-dog enclosure. Everyone there was understanding, helpful, and appropriately cautious. I learned a lot. I didn't even bark, growl, or lunge as each of five new dogs approached me one after another. Truth be told, I did hide behind Jeanne most of the time.

I was great at schmoozing with the humans, though. Guess I've already learned that from Bode.

We plan regular visits to Bark Park so I can gradually encounter many more unfamiliar dogs and their owners.

Love,

Lady

THE LOOK

Dear Diary,

Day 12. Today I got THE LOOK. I can't say that I liked it. When Jeanne gives it, you don't want it aimed at you. It means, from her eyes to yours, something to the effect of: you-will-be-in-huge-trouble-if-you-don't-do-what-you-know-I-want-you-to-do-NOW. It's sort of like sign language of the eyes.

You sure learn a bunch of new stuff around here every day. This morning, six thirty a.m. found us in a sit-stay at the end of the driveway, waiting for the monstrously loud behemoth that eats our garbage once a week. Last time it surprised me, and I was so frightened that I ran under the hedge. Now I'm a pro. That smelly old truck roared down our road today, hissing and gobbling at each and every trash can. I sat quietly and watched it—no barking, no hiding, nothing but mild interest. As it drove away, a man hanging off its back yelled to me that I'm a pretty dog!

After breakfast, Catcher—the two-year-old retriever who lives next door—and I had a little get-together to work on resolving some mutual aggression. Our meet and greet went well, consisting mainly of civilized sniffing and then a short walk together on leash. Neither of us showed so much as a drop of fear or loathing. I do hope we can be friends because Catcher has been missing out on all of my pack's trips and adventures. Besides, she loves to chase a ball, and Bode is such a fuddy-duddy when it comes to mindless play.

Last on our morning agenda, we had a lovely visit from Patrick (age ten) and James (nine), who were visiting their grandmother nearby. They rode over to our house on their bikes and agreed to help socialize me. I was surprised that they knew what the word "socialize" means. Evidently, their boxer named Dempsey has taught them how to act around all sorts of dogs, so I didn't feel in any way uneasy with them. But they talked so much that I had to lie down and take a nap!

Love,

Lady

James and Patrick socialize with Lady.

No Rest for the Weary

Dear Diary,

Day 13. The drill sergeant's golf match got rained out after nine holes, so my planned extended afternoon snooze went south.

Her backup plan was to do Media Day, which began with watching TV and videos. Sometimes dogs bark inside the big box. But I can't smell them or touch them, even when I lick the screen.

We also listened to some opera, although I seriously adore and much prefer Eric Clapton. The reading part of Media Day was more to my liking. In fact, I found Jeanne's book absolutely irresistible. She left the room to make more popcorn, and when she returned, she discovered that its cover was ever so slightly chewed off. I hoped she didn't think I had anything to do with it, but Lord knows "Perfect Boy Bode" would never have committed such a crime. Ne-ver. And (who knew?) it was a borrowed book, so there was considerable grumbling about ordering a replacement from Amazon .com. At times like this, I'm glad I'm a dog without a credit card.

Eventually it was suppertime—that is, Jeanne's suppertime. My most polite vocabulary word for this event is: sadism. She sat on the floor with her plate at the most exquisitely tempting level, just below nose high. *My* nose, that is. Tenderloin tips and broccoli and sweet potatoes. Instant drool. Well, not for the veggies. All through that torturous meal, I heard nothing but, "Leave it. Leave it. Leave it. Leave it . . ."

I hoped against hope that, at least once, I might hear, "Take it." No way. It took her what seemed like years to finish that plate of food. But I did manage to resist it.

Finally, it was *my* suppertime. Phew!
Love,
Lady

Lines Are Drawn

Dear Diary,

Day 14. Mantra du jour: "Out of the Kitchen."

When meals are being prepared, there's an imaginary line on the kitchen tile that dogs are not allowed to cross. Could this be a safety issue to prevent a certain someone from tripping over me with a hot TV dinner in her hands? (Yes, for a dog, I can be a little catty.) From my vantage point behind the back of his butt, I can see that Bode has a somewhat loose interpretation of this line. Well, it is imaginary . . .

All I want is to be close to the action in case some delicious morsel falls on the floor. Despite the "out of the kitchen" protocol, one time I even dared to try a little counter surfing. Did that ever get me THE LOOK—mega big-time!

Love,

Lady

Eating like a Lady

Dear Diary,

Day 15. Fourteen days have passed, and I got my two-week report card today.

Most important to the pack, I now will eat beside Bode without objection—even under the most trying circumstances. Jeanne switches our dishes' floor position in midstream, moves them from one part of the room to another, reverses the order in which we're fed, has us eat out of the same bowl, and makes us wait with a full dish in front of us.

I'm a little disappointed that she insists on staying in the room while we eat. "Just in case," she says. I guess restoring trust takes time.

Next week we plan to work on "bring dish." I will learn to bring it to Jeanne when I've finished eating. My reward will be petit square de mozzarella du jour, the premier treat around here.

The good news is that I raised my grade on nail filing with the Dremel from a D to a B-. Jeanne says that's humongous!

Each day we review and reinforce all that I've learned so far. Next week we'll concentrate on "sit," "down," and "stay," which I know I'll ace. (So much for what some people say about blondes!)

Love,
Lady

Lady tolerates a Dremel pedicure.

What's a Rhetorical Question?

Dear Diary,

Day 16. Today I learned about rhetorical questions. Apparently they don't require an answer, but I had one ready anyway.

Jeanne asked, "Do you know how frustrating it is to mop the floor with YOU following my every step?" In my head, I yelled, "No, I don't! First, I'm a dog. It's what we do. Second, my former residence was cleaned with a pressure hose. Until I came here, I'd never even heard of a Swiffer." So we agreed to work even harder on my down-stay in case another cleaning day rolls around soon. That command has many other vital uses, or so I'm told.

This afternoon I was greeted with one of the worst pieces of news I'd heard since my arrival: "We have to clean up because we're having company." Not to cast any aspersions, but I've lived in this pack for two weeks and this was the first time I'd ever met the vacuum cleaner. It didn't scare me one bit. Then again, I am justifiably terrified of the yellow feather duster.

Jeanne is making a sign to put on the basket of lint rollers we keep by the front door: "Three blondes live here, so just deal with the hair."

Love,
Lady

Party Hearty

Dear Diary,

Day 17. I attended my first people party last night. "Hey, look at me," I thought, "an outdoor dog lying under a dining room table while people sit, eat, drink, and laugh." I'd like to learn how to laugh. It looks like fun. Except for Jeanne, none of the partying people live with dogs. I could tell that from the first whiff. Although Jeanne had already briefed them on how to greet the new dog, I felt compelled to try a feeble bark or two. Then I got THE LOOK and quickly pulled myself together.

Bode advised that we should station ourselves underneath the table during dinner to see what might drop onto the floor. No food landed, but lots of interesting smells. I was hoping someone would slip off an uncomfy shoe for me to chew on, but no luck there either.

When they all retired to the living room, I stayed close to Jeanne. I know she was happy to have me near, but I think she was also wishing that I could have felt comfortable enough to work the room like Bode. Perfect Boy schmoozes like a politician, leaning into people to get petted and adored. I bet he would even kiss a baby. I hope that one day I'll be able to work the room confidently too.

Love,
Lady

Eat Your Heart Out, Rachael Ray

Dear Diary,

Day 18. This afternoon Jeanne and I played around in the kitchen. Here's my easy-peasy dog biscuit recipe. I found it on the Internet and tweaked it a bit to suit my own tasty specs. All of the ingredients are available at your local supermarket.

Lady's Peanut Butter Cookies:
2 cups peanut butter, creamy or crunchy—the kind with no soy (gluten)
1 cup milk—you can substitute lactose-free milk, or water, if desired
2+ cups instant potato flakes—100% real potatoes with no other ingredients

Cream the milk and peanut butter together, then mix in the potato flakes. Keep adding the potatoes until this forms an easy-to-work dough. Drop the "cookies" onto an ungreased baking sheet, using the small end of a melon ball tool to form a perfect-size dog biscuit. Bake at 375° for twenty minutes. Remove from baking sheet and cool on a wire rack. Store in fridge. "Serve them often," I tell my friends, "and eat your heart out!"

Love,
Lady

Enthralled by the Beach

Dear Diary,

Day 19. Today I fell hopelessly in love with the beach. Ecstasy! From the moment my paws hit the cool, moist sand for the first time, I was so busy seeing, smelling, and hearing the sights, scents, and sounds that I nearly forgot to notice all the new people and dogs I was meeting.

It was such a relief not to have any reason for fear aggression, especially since today is report card day for week three. I'd been sensing a low grade coming on in this department because Jeanne sometimes expects unprecedented miracles. I'm teaching her patience, though, and right now (truth be told) there's no way can she take home an A. But we're workin' on it.

Back to the beach. We met two special beings on our walk—Ronna and her Norwegian elkhound, Tess. They both know their dogs and approached me just the way I like it—slow, confident, and quiet. I could tell that Jeanne was thrilled with my calm response.

The beach is good. Life is good.

Love,

Lady

Bode and Lady rest in their chapel in the sand.

Charting for Success

Dear Diary,

Day 20. The drill sergeant says, "Enough with the dinner parties, recipes, and beach walks. It's time to implement phase two of our training plan." She's got charts on the fridge. She tells me what she's going to tell me. Then she tells me it. Then she tells me what she told me. Talk about military precision. Next she'll be singing Jody calls!

Our goal in phase two is to master all ten tasks required to pass the American Kennel Club's Canine Good Citizen (CGC) test. Whew! Ersatz Eagle Scouts for dogs? Although a CGC test is not required for a service dog, Jeanne thinks it will keep us focused on learning new things.

Passing this exam is a long-term goal, and Jeanne says the going might get tough, but we can make it. The CGC test will be administered by an AKC-certified evaluator. I'll have to wear a plain buckle collar, since training collars are not allowed. Some of the requirements will be especially challenging for me because I was not socialized as a puppy. Bring 'em on; I love to learn!

First task on the AKC list: Accepting a friendly stranger. According to the chart on our fridge, this demonstrates that I will allow a friendly stranger to approach me and speak to Jeanne in a natural, everyday situation. The evaluator and Jeanne will shake hands and exchange pleasantries. I must show no sign of resentment or shyness, and I must not break position or try to approach the evaluator.

Bode passed the CGC test a year ago, but Jeanne says he needs a tune-up, so we can all practice together.

Love,

Lady

Strangers Are Hard to Find

Dear Diary,

Day 21. Many AKC Canine Good Citizen test requirements call for strangers. Strangers to pat you, greet you, brush you, examine your ears, and check your teeth. We've run out of strangers on our street because in the early days of my arrival Jeanne was obsessed with introducing me to everyone within a one-hundred-mile radius.

First, she wanted them to know who I was, in case I got lost and couldn't find my way back home. She also wanted to begin socializing me. And she wanted to introduce people to Canine Angels. So now we've had to expand our operations to nearby streets to find strangers for practicing the test requirements.

Second on our list is to master Task 2: Sitting Politely for Petting. This demonstrates that I will allow a friendly stranger to touch me while I'm out and about with Jeanne. I must sit at Jeanne's side as the evaluator approaches and pets my head and body. I'm allowed to stand in place to accept petting. I must not show shyness or resentment.

Frankly, I suspect I could pass this requirement right now, but Jeanne insists on perfection. And admittedly, I can be a little hesitant when first confronted by people I haven't smelled before. I'm a hundred times more comfortable than I was two weeks ago, but I'm not yet what you'd call laid back. More work and more strangers coming up . . .

Love,
Lady

What a Girl Won't Do for a Cheese Cube

Dear Diary,

Day 22. In addition to daily reminders on Tasks 1 and 2 of the CGC, we've now moved ahead to Task 3: Appearance and Grooming. I'm supposed to welcome being groomed and examined. I must also permit a stranger, such as a veterinarian, groomer, or friend of Jeanne's, to check me out. This task also will reveal whether Jeanne takes good care of me. The evaluator will inspect me, comb or brush me, and lightly examine my ears and front feet.

Can't honestly say that I welcome being groomed, but what I do welcome is the cheese cube rewards I get for tolerating my beauty parlor sessions, as Jeanne calls them. She tries to make them fun, with lots of chatter. (What else is new?) She demonstrates the task on Bode while I watch. Then it's my turn.

That once grubby outdoor-pen girl now endures twice-weekly spa sessions with MalAcetic Otic ear cleanser and cotton balls, Dremel nail filer, chicken-flavored enzymatic toothpaste, and all manner of grooming brushes. And in the end, there's mozzarella!

Love,

Lady

Bode supervises Teeth Brushing 101.

Relinquish the Lead

Dear Diary,

Day 23. AKC CGC Task 4: Walking on a Loose Leash.

Jeanne must show that she's in full control of me. I can be on either side of her. There must be a left turn, a right turn, and an about-turn with at least one stop in between, and another turn at the end.

On any given day, my performance of this task has ranged from flawless to failing. So we practice, practice, practice. My service member and I will use this skill every day until forever.

Love,

Lady

Balk or Walk?

Dear Diary,

Day 24. Task 5: Walking through a Crowd.

I'm supposed to be able to move about politely in pedestrian traffic and behave well in public places. When tested, Jeanne and I must walk around and close to at least three strangers. I am permitted to show some interest in these people, but I must not become overly exuberant, shy, or resentful. Jeanne may talk to me and encourage or praise me throughout the test. I must not strain at the leash.

But I don't know if I'm ready. I don't want to put on that service-dog-in-training vest and go to a mall or public event until I'm really sure that I won't get overwhelmed. I would hate to give anyone a poor impression of me, of Jeanne, or of service dogs.

But it sure is a fine-looking vest.

Jeanne told me we would start this task slowly. Then she asked me to accompany her to a meeting of about fifty women golfers. This did not sound slow to me. Jeanne said the ladies would be so busy chatting, eating, and receiving awards that we could sneak in under the radar for some invaluable practice with less stress than at a crowded mall.

Turns out that we had fun. I didn't escape notice by any means, but the ladies

Lady perfects her party posture during a women's golf league event.

were encouraging and full of compliments. And they even asked for permission to pat me. I behaved so well that it brought tears to Jeanne's eyes. Go figure . . .

I don't want you to think it was easy, though. At first, all the noise and milling about was a bit tough to endure. When they applauded the tournament winners, I jumped. But I didn't try to run. And I certainly never growled, cowered, or barked. While my tail was a little tucked under, every time I was asked to "say hello" to someone, I faced them politely and calmly accepted pats on the head.

Did I ever collapse with exhaustion when we got home!

Love,

Lady

Say Hello to Joe

Dear Diary,

Day 25. Today I want to introduce my "foster brother," Joe, also known as USAF Major Joe Maxon. I haven't actually met him in person because he's currently deployed to the Persian Gulf. Apparently Lulu can't drive us there.

I've seen his picture on Jeanne's bureau, and I've heard lots of stories about Joe. I even got to sniff the beautiful big plant he sent us on Mother's Day.

Joe would love to have a dog, but his military career sends him away from home far too much, often on extremely short notice. So he was especially interested when Jeanne volunteered to foster and train me to enable a veteran in need. He was so interested, in fact, that he donated $1,000 to Canine Angels. This gift is to support my care and feeding during training, as well as that of my other canine colleagues who will go on to serve an individual who so honorably served our nation.

I love Joe because Jeanne does, and also because I can smell a caring and compassionate being a zillion miles away. Thank you, Joe.

Love,

Lady

Why Go "Cheese-less?"

Dear Diary,

Day 26. Task 6: Sit and Down on Command. Staying in Place.

This test demonstrates that I've had training through my response to Jeanne's commands "sit" and "down," and remaining where placed.

Jeanne will be allowed a reasonable amount of time and may use more than one command to make me sit and then lie down. When instructed by the evaluator, Jeanne will tell me to stay and then will walk forward the length of a twenty-foot line. I must remain in place, although I may change position.

Now, I'm not one to brag, but I've practiced this task a lot, so I think I can phone in at least a B+ on this week's report card. I did leave my assigned place a few times to check out some tempting distractions, but then Jeanne would take me back to try again. Voila! It worked. I've still got a few days to bring home an A.

One thing she's been reminding me of is that, when we do feel ready to take the AKC CGC test, we will not be allowed to use treats to entice or re-ward behavior. No matter how spectacular I am, no mozzarella will change hands—not even so much as a cube.

I must say, you don't need practice to be miserable, so why bother with-holding treats until it's absolutely necessary? So far Jeanne is in agreement, but I don't know how long my luck will hold out. Here's hoping we don't go "cheese-less" any time soon.

Love,

Lady

It Seems So Simple . . .

Dear Diary,

Day 27. Task 7: Coming When Called.

I've heard that this is the most sought-after dog behavior. I'd like to have a dollar for every time a dog owner has lamented to Jeanne, "If only he/she would come when I call." We'd collect a bundle and give it to dog welfare groups.

Task 7 seems simple enough. It demonstrates that I will come when called. Having told me to stay, Jeanne will walk ten feet away from me, turn to face me, and then call me. She may use encouragement to get me to come.

We decided to start small, with me on leash and Jeanne going only about five feet away. Next, she'll call me enthusiastically and tug on the leash. When I get to her, she'll heap on lots of praise (and cheese, of course)! Then we'll repeat, repeat, and repeat. Sometimes Bode participates in these sessions, but I can tell he's only in it for the treats.

For a while, Jeanne was feeling quite smug when I would return to her on command while off leash at the beach. What she forgot to remember was that I was returning because I wanted to. The real test is for me to return when I don't want to—like when I'm contemplating chasing a bird, bunny, or squirrel.

So we still need the leash and the cheese and the encouragement and the practice, practice, practice.

Love,

Lady

**Lady enjoys cavorting in a huge alfalfa field
before "coming when called."**

Behaving like a Lady

Dear Diary,

Day 28. Task 8: Reaction to Another Dog.

This task demonstrates that I can behave politely around other dogs. During the test, Jeanne and I will be approached by another dog/handler team. We will stop, allowing the two handlers to exchange pleasantries, and then continue on. I must show no more than a casual interest in the other dog.

Frankly, this is one of my biggest improvements since joining our pack. Four weeks ago, I would freak out when confronted with an unfamiliar dog—jumping, squealing, barking, and pulling hard on my leash. Not a pretty sight. I was scared silly and was doing a pretty good job of scaring the other dog's owner.

But by now I've met so many new dogs that I'm almost always indifferent to them. Jeanne says that's perfect! I have definitely nailed this task. More mozzarella, please.

Love,

Lady

Lightning Strikes

Dear Diary,

Day 29. Last I had heard, we planned to spend thirty minutes or so reviewing Tasks 1 through 8 of the AKC CGC test. But the moment we headed out the front door, we were met with black skies, heavy rain, thunder, and lightning.

I figured I was off the hook. Nope. There was a Plan B. We retreated to the screened porch to keep us safe during the storm. While this wasn't my favorite environment, I sat angelically by the kitchen door and waited for Jeanne to regain her senses. I'd give myself a B+ for tolerating all that booming and flashing. On the other hand, Jeanne was flinching visibly at every lightning strike. I'm thinking we pencil in a C- for her and give us each a cheese cube.

Love,
Lady

Reaction to Distractions

Dear Diary,

Day 30. To pass Task 9, I'm supposed to be confident when faced with common distractions, such as the dropping of a large book or a jogger running in front of me. I'm allowed to be interested or curious, and can even appear slightly startled. I must not panic, try to run away, show aggression, or bark.

I heard that when Bode took the test, the evaluator stood behind him and dropped two stainless steel bowls onto the concrete from a height of about four feet. Perfect Boy's only reaction was to turn his head and look utterly bored.

So maybe I've got some work to do on this task.

As you might have guessed, right now we're headed to Walmart to buy some stainless steel bowls. If only Jeanne would take me into the store so I could sneak some earplugs into the cart.

Love,

Lady

Loving the Links

Dear Diary,

Day 31. I played my first nine holes this afternoon with Jeanne. I hope this was the first of many such wonderful outings. I love golf and totally adore riding in the cart!

We checked in at the pro shop where I met lots of new people, smelled a bunch of merchandise, and then proceeded to the bag drop. I willingly climbed onto the cart seat and rode shotgun while Jeanne drove. I quickly grew accustomed to her driving style and learned how to brace myself when she yelled, "Hold on."

The rules say that I have to stay off the greens and sand traps, and remain in the cart when so instructed. Oh yes, I must not snort or snicker if Jeanne hits a poor shot. Since I'm new to the game, I wouldn't know a good shot from a bad one, but I am quite capable of reading body language. Suffice it to say, there was some pretty revealing body language going on during those nine holes. Being polite, I looked the other way.

Golf lingo is also new to me. At one point I had trouble figuring out whether Jeanne was talking to me or the ball when she muttered, "Sit." Since I was already prone on the cart seat, I assumed she was addressing the ball. Later on, I figured out that a certain golf word rhyming with "sit" can only be said under one's breath at the risk of earning penalty strokes.

While it may seem that the pack was playing hooky on the links this afternoon, I was actually being tested on most of the ten AKC CGC tasks without even knowing it. Hardest of all was ignoring the many birds, squirrels, and turtles that crossed our path during the round.

If my adopting service member is a golfer, or would like to be, I'll be ready.

Love,

Lady

Golf terms and etiquette are critical to Lady's training in the event she's placed with a veteran who enjoys the links.

How Long Is Three Minutes?

Dear Diary,

Day 32. I just checked my training chart that lives on the fridge. It's hard to believe, but by now I've been introduced to all ten of the AKC Canine Good Citizen test requirements. I haven't mastered all of them, but I know I will.

The final one, Task 10, is called Supervised Separation. I'm supposed to show my good manners by tolerating being left with a trusted person. The evaluator will say something to the effect of, "Would you like me to watch your dog?" and will take my leash. Then Jeanne will go out of sight for three minutes. I don't have to stay in position, but I must not show any behavior stronger than mild agitation.

I think I'll need a watch and to learn how to tell time. Three minutes doesn't seem long, except when you're hanging by your fingernails, that is. Why does Jeanne have to go away, and where exactly will she be? Out of scent range? I hope not. Will the person I'm entrusted to have mozzarella? Will they know how I like my ears massaged? Will they talk to me?

This could be unsettling, but I suppose we'll approach it like everything else—practice, practice, practice. I sure hope the trusted person practices being trusty.

Love,

Lady

Luck Be a Lady

Dear Diary,

Day 33. Words cannot describe my ecstasy.

From the moment I stepped off the dock and onto the deck of the Century speedboat, I was in heaven. This boat goes way faster than a golf cart, and you can even stand on the bow with the wind streaming through your hair just like Kate Winslet in *Titanic*.

When we slowed down, I found that I was nose to beak with the most amazing variety of water fowl. Fascinating—and more than a little tempting . . .

Then we cut engine and set anchor (note my new nautical vocabulary), and I jumped out for a swim. Delightful! I've never dared to venture into the water on our daily beach walks. But on this day I was fearless.

I am a lucky girl to have all these learning opportunities, and I will be forever grateful.

Love,

Lady

When I Am Old and Gray

Dear Diary,

Day 34. I've met many different fellow canines since I joined this pack. Some took a little getting used to. Some I liked right away. Some I simply chose to treat with indifference.

There are a few, though, whom I admire with all my heart. They have courage, strength, and grace under fire. I can smell it.

Let me tell you about two of them.

First, there's my friend Ginger. She's a vivacious, nearly eleven-year-old chocolate lab. She's got a contagious wiggle and an endearing way of snuggling up to you. I bet she's hardly ever met a person she didn't instantly accept and like without question.

But severe arthritis is robbing Ginger of the ability to flush out squirrels, birds, and all the other critters so tempting to her breed. Jumping in and out of the car and even climbing the bedroom stairs pose daily challenges. Because, as we all know, certain drugs prescribed for arthritis pain can adversely affect the liver and cause other complications, Ginger has been introduced to acupuncture to alleviate her pain. The jury is still out on whether she'll feel relief, but we are hopeful. And she goes with the flow, regardless. She is way cool.

Another of my friends has diabetes. She's a foxy black-and-white springer spaniel named Belle, age thirteen. Diabetes left Belle blind, so she endured a lens replacement in her right eye (for distance) and cataract removal in the left (for reading). This surgery was a godsend because Belle is also deaf, and a dog that can neither see nor hear would be easy prey.

The years have also affected Belle's legs. Her right hip joint had to be disconnected surgically due to dysplasia, and her left hip joint crater simply disappeared over time. As if that weren't enough, her front leg has six pins in it from a boating accident suffered long ago.

Despite a daily regimen of insulin and other medications, Belle retains her sweet and gentle nature. She loves everyone—people and animals alike. She is a real southern belle. Paws down, she is the kind of girlfriend I'd invite to go through my toy chest any day of the week.

It's an honor to know Ginger and Belle. And I am comforted. Jeanne tells me my adopting veteran will be screened to ensure that he or she will care for me with the same kind of love and attention. That is, when I am old and gray.

Love,

Lady

Surprise, Surprise!

Dear Diary,

Day 35. This week we made a visit to a major department store to hone my public appearance skills. Before entering the store aisles, Jeanne advised me that we needed to make a short detour to the ladies' restroom.

The handicapped stall (roomy enough for both of us and convenient for keeping me in sight) was empty, so we stepped in. A quick reconnaissance of the cubicle revealed no visible temptations, such as errant squares of toilet paper or other debris on the floor. Then Jeanne turned her back to close the door, slide the lock, and hang her purse on the hook. Mistake, leaving me to my own devices like that for so much as a split second.

Before she could turn around, a loud shriek emanated from the adjacent stall. Yikes! All I did was belly-crawl a teensy bit under the stall partition to smell the shoe that was positioned there. At first I wasn't even aware that there was a foot, a leg, and a whole woman attached to the shoe. That is, until the shrieking. Needless to say, I beat the world record for belly-crawling backward.

Lord knows, I have a shoe fetish. I fetch shoes from Jeanne's closet at least five times a day. So it seemed reasonable to me to check this one out, too.

From that one quick sniff I did learn a little about that poor,

Left to her own devices for a second, Lady surprises a "stall mate."

startled woman. She's not too comfortable around dogs, especially ones whose heads suddenly appear beneath the partition of a public bathroom stall. Jeanne surmised that, judging from her sensible tan laced-up shoes and support hose, she might be either elderly or someone who works on her feet. Maybe not the kind of lady to find anything funny about my sudden appearance.

After repeated, profuse, heartfelt apologies through the partition, the lady said she was okay, so Jeanne and I fled like a couple of bandits. We marched all the way over to the toy section before stopping to apply our hand sanitizer. Never did see that lady's face.

Since Jeanne is taking the blame for this one, I'm not in the doghouse. But our public restroom procedures are definitely under revision.

Love,

Lady

O Ye of Little Faith

Dear Diary,

Day 36. Last night Jeanne was in the midst of dinner preparations. We were having a small three-pack celebration in honor of the Golden Angels learning to jump through a hoop, literally.

Cooking sounds and smells from our kitchen are woefully unusual, so this generated a great deal of interest from Bode and me. A roasted boneless turkey breast was resting, as some who actually know how to cook might say, on the kitchen counter.

Then the phone rang. On the other end, our beach-walking, dog-loving friend Ronna asked Jeanne tearfully, "Can you meet me at my vet's?"

"Be there in ten minutes," she responded. No questions asked.

Knowing that Ronna's gorgeous Norwegian elkhound, Tess, is a cancer survivor and suffers other serious health issues, we were scared.

Our usual "desperately quick exit" checklist includes: have Bode and I been out for a pee recently? All else can be tolerated or remedied. That said and done, we unhappy campers were advised that dinner would have to wait, and we were to "stay."

After an hour of exams, tests, and consults, the good news was that Tess's gastrointestinal distress could be fixed with assorted shots, pills, and credit cards. Whew. Throughout this ordeal, a fragrant turkey rested on our kitchen counter. Two hungry goldens. No supervision.

When she recalled the scenario, Jeanne said she was relieved that at least it was a boneless turkey, though she wondered what sort of gastrointestinal event three pounds of turkey could possibly serve up. Isn't turkey supposed to make you sleepy? Don't panic if you walk in and find two snoring golden beauties, she thought.

When she pulled into the garage and dashed in the house, there we were—sitting angelically side by side at the laundry room door. The look on our faces bespoke induction into the most exalted ranks of sainthood. Yet, she said she almost didn't want to proceed around the corner to the kitchen.

Tune in tomorrow for a report on the Great Turkey Caper—written either from a time-out or while splayed next to the French doors enjoying the rays and praise.

Love,

Lady

Basking, or Jailed?

Dear Diary,

Day 37. Referencing yesterday's diary entry: All those who think that Bode and I ate the roasted turkey that sat on the edge of our kitchen counter for two hours please raise your hands.

It *was* suppertime and we *were* unsupervised and we are *not* usually tested with the aroma of roasted anything emanating from our kitchen. It would be understandable to give in to the temptation, don't you think?

But I am so proud to report that the turkey breast was untouched when Jeanne flew in the door after her trip to Tess's vet. No time-outs for this duo. Bode and I are *so* basking in the rays and praise at the French doors.

Love,

Lady

In Honor of Those Who Serve

Dear Diary,

Day 38. Memorial Day is an especially important holiday for my Canine Angels pack. Much of the time and effort we expend as volunteers is in honor or memory of the men and women who have served our country. Now I am working twice as hard as before to be ready to serve in my own way.

This Memorial Day is even more special to me because it marks my first acquaintance with a decorated veteran of World War II. I am honored to introduce my friend, Bob Bradicich, who served as a rifleman with the 28th Infantry Division in Europe from 1943 to 1945.

He was only eighteen when his combat team landed at Omaha Beach. They fought their way through France and across the Siegfried Line into Germany and the Battle of the Bulge. Bob brought home two medals earned through his bravery: the Bronze Star and the Purple Heart. He also brought home memories of the horrors of war that would haunt him throughout the years to come.

So, on this stately holiday weekend, I will be thinking of Bob and countless others whose selfless service ensures our freedom today.

Next Memorial Day, I hope that my fellow Canine Angels and I are also in your thoughts as we serve our adopting veterans.

Love,

Lady

**Bob Bradicich is a decorated WWII veteran
who befriended Lady.**

The Pack Is on Full Alert

Dear Diary,

Day 39. After a holiday weekend of peaceful reflection punctuated by the mouthwatering scent of hot dogs on our grill, the proverbial party is over and the drill sergeant is back on duty.

Right after reveille at five thirty this morning, we heeled off leash to the mailbox, picked up and didn't shy from that noisy trash barrel, and ignored upon stern command a couple of squirrels rudely thrashing about in the bushes.

The reason behind this renewed basic training vigor is exciting: my AKC Canine Good Citizenship test has been scheduled. It's just two weeks away, and am I ever wired!

I thought I had dodged a bullet when at first there were no test evaluators close to where we live. No such luck. Instantly, Jeanne got on the computer and phone, refusing to take no for an answer (even though she constantly expects me to do so). She finally found a scheduled test in nearby Wilmington, and made plans to pack up the three-pack and move off on D-day.

By then I will have lived in this pack for two months. Perfect Boy had to train for six months before he took his test. And he hadn't lived in a chain-link pen for the first two years of his life. What I'm getting at here is that there's a chance I could fail.

I know that this milestone is utterly important to Jeanne, so I will do my absolute best. She insists that she'll still love me with all her heart, regardless of the result. (I know this is true because yesterday when I rolled in dog poop, jumped up, and shook it onto her new golf outfit, she didn't stop loving me.)

All I know now is that day passes and leaves are cancelled and my pack is on something like full alert.

Love,

Lady

Bode takes an up-close look at Lady's test requirements.

Can You Blame a Girl for Trying?

Dear Diary,

Day 40. I'm forever being asked to bring something. "Bring dish (after I eat) . . . bring bone . . . bring ball . . ." If it isn't one dang thing, it's another.

I figured I could get a jump-start on this requirement. With the big test coming up and all, I thought it would be smart to be proactive. So I started bringing things even before being asked. How cool is that?

The first thing I chose was Jeanne's new sandal, which was lying listlessly on the closet floor. That was not a hit. Nor was the shower bathmat, which I brought next. My worst idea, apparently, was the quilt off our bed. I pranced out triumphantly with these items between my teeth and was met with THE LOOK, followed by a loudly cleared throat.

I get the picture. It's like the magnet on our fridge says: "My name is 'No, No! Bad Dog!' What's yours?"

Love,

Lady

A New Challenge Considered

Dear Diary,

Day 41. Wearing my service-dog-in-training vest proudly, I thought we were simply enjoying a Memorial Day ceremony at the VFW. Bagpipes, fire engine sirens, screechy microphones, applause, crowds, pats from strangers—I wasn't a bit shy about any of it.

But I should have known that my pack leader is never really off duty and absolutely never misses an opportunity to torment me. So she immediately noticed that some of the senior veterans we honored were using canes, walkers, wheelchairs, oxygen, and other medical aids.

Apparently, a light was switched on in her military mind which caused her to ramble on all the way home about some so-called therapy dog test. It seems that mastering a few additional requirements beyond those of the AKC Canine Good Citizen test could certify me as a therapy dog.

I'm like, "Come on. I haven't even mastered the ten AKC tasks yet."

"It's just five more," she implored.

"I don't know. Five more tasks on top of *ten* AKC requirements?"

"It's all included in the same test," she whined, "and it would just mean ten or so more minutes."

As I understand it, here's the "more" she's asking of me:

- <u>Reaction to Medical Equipment.</u> I must walk around wheelchairs, walkers, canes, and crutches to make sure I'm not nervous about them.
- <u>Leave It.</u> I must walk—on loose lead—past a plate of food on the ground and ignore it when told "Leave it." Perfect Boy had to step

around a plate of bacon bits on his test! Jeanne admitted that even she was tempted by the bacon, but Bode did leave it. I'm starting to admire that guy. Maybe I'll stop calling him Perfect Boy. This task is important in case someone in my vicinity should drop medicine, medical waste, or anything else that might be hazardous to my health. We must be sure I'll "leave it" when it really matters.

- Accepting Infirmities. I would have to be confident and calm when exposed to people walking with an uneven gait, shuffling, breathing heavily, coughing, sneezing, or demonstrating any other distraction I might encounter in a medical facility.
- Say Hello. No, I'm not required to actually speak, and for that I am thankful. That's probably next month. "Say hello" means I'm supposed to show willingness to visit with a person and make myself accessible for petting.
- Reaction to Children. They will closely watch my reaction toward children playing, running, or just standing around. Any negative reaction will result in automatic failure. No sign of aggression will be tolerated.

Truth be told, I'm already fairly comfortable with most of these requirements. Avoiding the plate of bacon seems a bit much, but we all know that I love to please. So yes, I've agreed to try for the therapy dog certification in addition to the AKC Canine Good Citizen.

What can I say? I'm a golden.

Love,

Lady

Countdown to Testing

Dear Diary,

Day 42. A certain pack leader who shall remain nameless has just gone around the bend into manic mode. Test day was "T minus six" and counting.

To test my reaction to distractions (Task 9), books were flying off shelves and slamming down onto the floor with a life of their own like objects in a Harry Potter movie. Julia Child's cookbook weighs at least four pounds and could terrify a rock when it crashes onto a tile floor. But this didn't scare me. Onward!

There could be as many as twenty-four other dog candidates at the test. So, because I've occasionally been unsettled around some dogs, Jeanne loaded us up and sped us to the local dog park for socialization practice. Not a soul was there, maybe because it was nearly ninety degrees. Her frustration was so palpable that I could smell it, so we sped back there for another try a few hours later. No dice. By then it was ninety-three. Now I'm told that a play date has been arranged for tomorrow morning. Task 8 will not go away.

In keeping with the tinge of panic in the air, we combined Tasks 1 and 2 into Accepting a Friendly Stranger and Sitting Politely for Petting. Several kind folks at the golf pro shop helped with these tasks. These strangers of yesterday are now my friends of today and forever. Thanks, guys.

Love,

Lady

Scrambling for Charity

**Fitting comfortably in a golf cart is a snap
for Bode and Lady.**

Dear Diary,

Day 43. Yesterday marked yet another new experience. I played in my
first charity golf tournament. It was a scramble format, and I was on a team
with Jeanne, Bode, and three of our friends. A "scramble" (check out my
new golf lingo) is when the team members each tee off and then go to play
from the location of the best shot. It continues that way through all eighteen
holes.

I was amazing, if I don't say so myself. The ladies in my "six-some" said
I was so well behaved that they hardly knew I was there. When they made
a birdie, I would leap out of the cart and dance around while they did
high-fives. If they only made a par, I would stay in the cart, look around

as though on squirrel watch, and yawn. Sad to say, there were more yawns than high-fives, although we had tons of laughs and smiles for the entire eighteen holes.

When we weren't running along behind Jeanne's golf cart, Bode and I took turns riding with each of the other ladies. They all wanted us in their carts, so we made sure to share the wealth. Speaking of wealth, the proceeds from this tournament went to Canine Angels! This golf league, of which I am a proud member, sponsors a tournament once a quarter to raise money for a local charity.

Because we were the beneficiary, the boss and a subpack of Canine Angels pups also played in the tournament. Apparently, they had fewer yawns and more high-fives than our team and came in second. We were third. Bode told me he suspected that Jeanne was a little miffed at losing a friendly wager with the boss. I didn't notice it, but of course, Bode has had his share of experience with these issues. I'll be watching for those side bets at my next scramble.

Love,

Lady

Social Butterflies Are Okay

Dear Diary,

Day 44. I've been notified that this week we will review and practice Task 8 (Reaction to Another Dog). I'm okay with this, but is it possible to get oversocialized? I certainly hope not.

On the beach this morning we met two Cavalier King Charles spaniels who ran around so fast and furious that they literally became a blur. Jeanne said that they were like whirling dervishes. I'm not sure whether I should repeat that since I don't know if it's PC (politically correct). The best we could do was to wave a polite hello and move on.

An abbreviated playgroup in my yard was next, with Justice visiting to play some ball. His official breed is American Staffordshire terrier, the formal name for pit bull. Jeanne trained him before she met me and already knew that he was a sweet and smart gentleman. We had a delightful afternoon.

In a couple of days I'm going to SOAR (Southport–Oak Island Animal Rescue), where I will meet and greet dozens of new canine friends. I think they also have cats roaming free there. I'm penciling them in on my social calendar.

Jeanne is golfing today, so Bode and I have the afternoon off. Thanks be to the Scots for inventing golf and giving the weary some rest.

T minus five and counting!

Love,

Lady

A Girlish Figure

Dear Diary,

Day 45. On top of all my training requirements, I'm told that I must maintain a girlish figure. This is not about vanity. We golden girls simply have to watch our weight.

When I joined this pack, I tipped the scale at a not-so-svelte seventy-one. I didn't have face folds (thank you, thank you, dog gods), but my waistline was clearly not in evidence and the jury was out as to the existence of ribs. Well, we returned from the vet an hour ago, and I'm delighted to report that over the last eight weeks I dropped a total of five-and-a-half pounds! Smokin'—eat your heart out, Jenny C.!

Most important, keeping lean and fit helps prevent heart and joint problems, stave off diabetes, and lower the odds for cancer. It also keeps my energy level high. Lord knows, gotta have energy to keep up with this pack. And it's common knowledge that goldens are prone to hip problems. Being overweight definitely ratchets up the potential risk surrounding these issues.

I think Jeanne is a bit jealous of my slimming success. She whines that if she had a personal trainer and dietician like mine, she too could lose a few pounds. But even if I knew how much she weighs, I certainly wouldn't publish it anywhere, let alone here.

Lest you think we forgot—T minus four and counting!

Love,

Lady

SOARing High

Dear Diary,

Day 46. Today my socialization reached a new level when I visited SOAR (Southport–Oak Island Animal Rescue) and met several shelter dogs who are looking for a forever home. Dogs and cats galore! I'm proud to say that I reacted beautifully, sometimes aloof, sometimes interested, and always Lady-like. Jeanne was impressed. Task 9 (Reaction to Another Dog)—I've got your number!

I don't know any of the cats' names, but I got up close and personal with three shelter dogs who are learning skills that will help make them more adoptable. Before the day was over, I had rubbed elbows with Homer, Trixie, and Pender from SOAR.

Homer has been at SOAR for five years, and some say he's "unadoptable." But I think of him as a brindle prince—well-mannered with no aggression whatsoever—a true aristocrat who would be happy to be a loving member of any pack. Trixie is a pit bull with shiny, jet-black hair. She is as strong as an ox and expresses her exuberant personality through a barrage of excited licks. Pender is a sweet-faced little black-and-tan mix who is happy to linger on the fringe of the pack, yet comes willingly when called. These pups are thriving due to the individual and group therapy sessions provided by Canine Angels. I wish each and every one a forever home as soon as can be.

At suppertime tonight we're headed to Walmart to review Task 5 (Walking through a Crowd).

T minus three and counting!

Love,

Lady

Girls Go Shopping

Dear Diary,

Day 47. I made my first shopping visit to Walmart today. It was awesome! There's an aisle dedicated entirely to cheese, all temptingly displayed at nose level. Mozzarella heaven! But I'm getting ahead of myself.

First, we were greeted at those magic automatic doors by a smiling octogenarian. Not sure, but I think that means a person with false teeth. She wished me a good visit and asked if I was in training. I thought this was a bit lame since at the time I was executing a perfect "heel." Jeanne mentioned that the lady might have read "In Training" on my service vest. Fair enough.

Jeanne seemed fairly annoyed with our shopping cart. "Would it be too much to ask to get a cart, just once, with four wheels that can turn, and all in the same direction?" I surmised that this was another one of those rhetorical questions she's famous for. No comment. So we struggle and make a lot of noise and can't sneak up on anyone. Big deal.

As we proceeded down a main aisle, I got lots of smiles from passersby. After all, I was wearing my purple vest, purple scarf, purple leash, and purple collar. Way chic. Pretty in purple, and do I ever like to strut my stuff.

Since it was my first shopping experience, we decided to keep it short. I was given a ten-dollar expense account, a veritable fortune for a chain-link-fence girl. In the boring battery aisle we got some new ones for our flashlight. Nothing caught my eye.

Then we headed straight to the cheese section. Without hesitation, I chose a two-pound mozzarella block—the largest I have ever seen. I realize that I must be "cheese-less" until after the big test, but when that fridge door opens on "T" day, my reward will be waiting on the shelf. Win or lose, I'll have earned that cheese.

The checkout counter came next. If I observed this correctly: we give the checkout lady our food, then she gives it back to us in a bag that we eventually use to pick up dog poop on our walks. They call this "recycling." A small rectangular plastic card changed hands briefly. Clearly, a lady need not concern herself with money, but I did notice that there was a dollar thirty-two left over for our next Walmart outing. That ought to be good for at least a little mozzarella.

T minus two, my friends.

Love,

Lady

I Love My Team

Dear Diary,

Day 48. Tomorrow is test day. I will do the best I can.

I'm cautiously optimistic, but if I don't succeed, I will on my next try. Whatever happens, I will always be grateful for having had this chance to be all that I can be. And I want to tell my family and friends something that is important to me. It's how much your encouragement, love, and support have sustained me through this stretch of my journey.

Gladys Knight nailed how I feel in her song "Best Thing That Ever Happened to Me."

Love,

Lady

Way Early on Test Day

Dear Diary,

Day 49. I hope my good buds are enjoying a peaceful cup of coffee as they read about this auspicious occasion. There is absolutely nothing remotely resembling peace surrounding my pack this morning.

Jeanne is nearly apoplectic with nerves, but I'm told she'll "cowgirl up" like the best of them when we get to the test.

Bode is sulking mightily since he's been advised that he won't be joining us for the trip to Wilmington. He'd be a great comfort to both Jeanne and me, but only handlers and contestants are allowed in the testing facility, and it will be too hot for him to wait in the Subaru.

Me, I could feel the tension in the air as early as yesterday. Had I thumbs, I could have cut it with a knife. So for some comic relief, I retrieved a roll of toilet paper from the counter and tore it to shreds. (Just thought I'd like to have the confetti ready and waiting.) Then I decided to eat half of it. This didn't elicit much of a laugh. Instead, it led to a prayer vigil regarding "this, too, will pass" by test time.

By now Lulu is packed and ready to leave an hour earlier than necessary. "Just in case," Jeanne says. That must be why we've loaded up enough food, water, medical records, leashes, and maps to support a cross-country migration. "Just in case."

We expect to be finished by one p.m. and will report to you tomorrow via *Lady Gram*. Thanks so much for all your support. I can practically smell your positive thoughts.

Love,
Lady

Break Out the Mozzarella!

Dear Diary,

Day 50. WE PASSED! (*A thunderous sigh of relief from us all . . .*)

The last task of the fifteen tested was Supervised Separation for three minutes. Jeanne left the building and paced around for our longest three minutes in history. When she returned, I was sitting angelically exactly where she had left me. Way to go! Pass!

The evaluator walked over to Jeanne, shook her hand, and said, "Congratulations, you have a therapy dog." Jeeze-Louise, if she didn't start crying—my tough drill sergeant in tears. Even the evaluator was dewy-eyed. She knew how much this meant to us. The scent of emotion in that room could have been bottled by Chanel.

Lots of paperwork changed hands, and then we were done. I got a totally chic CGC patch and a delicious cookie shaped like a blue ribbon. Jeanne would have liked to take a picture of it, but I wolfed it down as quick as I could. Was I ever starving by then! Jeanne treated me to a cheeseburger on the way home.

The evaluator made a special comment on my report card that said I was "calm, well mannered, sweet." Ain't it the truth?

Love,

Lady, AKC Canine Good Citizen/Therapy Dog

Laurels Not to Rest On

Dear Diary,

Day 51. Raise your hand if you think I was allowed to rest on my laurels for so much as a day? Not. This morning, with eyes barely open, I was briefed on our new training plan. Something about "raising the bar"...

Take it, bring it, leave it, heel off leash, give me five. The list is endless, and our work is cut out for us. Truth is, Jeanne will make it fun, and I love the challenge of learning and seeing her enthusiasm when I get it right.

I'll be so busy that I'll have to cut back my daily diary entries. I'll still be thinking of you all every day, but we're going to be consumed with our focus on performance (mine) and patience (Jeanne's). Will keep you posted.

Love,

Lady

An Unsung Hero

Dear Diary,

I've received tons of accolades recently for passing the Canine Good Citizen and Therapy Dog tests. Many of our friends and acquaintances have emailed, written on the website, and phoned to congratulate me. I even got a new boomerang toy and a box of yummy treats. All this attention is utterly flattering.

Yet, amid all the hoopla, I nearly forgot to acknowledge one of my greatest supporters—my packmate, Bode. Without a doubt, I never could have progressed as quickly without his help. Bode is the epitome of generosity and compassion. From the moment I came through his front door, he graciously shared Jeanne's devotion, his space on the big bed (except for first pick), seating and nose position at the open window when we ride in Lulu, and free access to his toy and bone box. About the only thing he won't budge on is his breakfast and dinner. No way! Well, a girl can't have everything.

I honestly believe that much of my success on this journey has been due to Bode's stellar example. When Jeanne gives a command that I don't fully understand, Bode is right there to translate it and show me what to do. Then I copycat him. When she's on the warpath, he lets me hide under the table by his side. When she's investigating who may have done a certain misdeed, he gives me permission to claim that maybe it wasn't me. When I have to go to the vet, he comes too, so I won't be scared. When the doorbell rings and we run to see who's there, sometimes he lets me win the race.

Even when I'm being a pesky younger sister, he tolerates my antics with Buddha-like patience. You have to love this boy. I sure do.

Love,

Lady

Bode and Lady pose for the family holiday card.

Happy Father's Day, Dad

Dear Diary,

I never knew my dad. Odds are, my mother met him only once. Since I'm a rescued dog, Jeanne didn't know him either. She says, though, that we ought to honor him today because he helped make me who I am. I like to think that I have him to thank, at least in part, for eyes like warm brown cognac and an enviably lush, feathery, blonde coat that's as soft as chinchilla on top of my head.

Maybe he also gave me the joy I have in living, my innate intelligence, and the way I love to learn.

Jeanne says I have the heart of a lion, but I don't think my dad was a lion. I guess it's just another one of her peculiar expressions.

Anyhow, in honor of Father's Day we spent yesterday celebrating Dad-style. We watched U.S. Open golf on TV and then we cooked hot dogs on the grill. Man-heaven.

Happy Father's Day, Dad!

Love,

Lady

Fun, Fitness, and a Fan

Dear Diary,

The "dog days of summer" find me triple-tasking. I discovered a perfect way to beat the heat, have fun, and stay fit—all at the same time. Swimming!

I snort with delight as I paddle about effortlessly, holding my head high above the water. The rest of me is blissfully submerged in the clear, calm, and lukewarm waters of the Atlantic. Sometimes I make huge splashes with my paws and try to bite the water. Jeanne laughs out loud as she digs her heels into the wet sand to withstand the ebb and flow at the water's edge.

Note that, while I'm swimming and having all this fun, I'm also doing non-weight-bearing exercise to strengthen my movement muscles. Jeanne says that this will definitely help lessen the aches and pains of aging down the road.

A word to the wise: If you swim in salt water, do not drink it. Be sure to have a large bowl of fresh water available. Even so, ocean water sometimes gets in your mouth, especially when you try to bite it. If you swallow it, it just may come right back up. This can be embarrassing.

Last best part about swimming is that you might be allowed to sit on the bow of the boat and speed along with the wind blowing through your hair like a giant fan. Best hair dryer ever invented.

I'm a lucky dog!

Love,

Lady

House Arrest

Dear Diary,

It's not what you think.

I definitely did not run amuck, so there's no explanation for the notice-able limp on my right front leg. Maybe I overdid the jumping in and out of the boat the other day. Now I've got a bit of joint pain.

So I'm on limited duty while we give my leg a rest. No beach walks, ball fetching, running squirrels, or jumping in and out of Lulu. Snuggling up with the heating pad is about my speed and feels really good. The only exercise I'm permitted is the walk to and from my food and water dishes.

Fortunately, Jeanne knows my habits and behavior so well that she im-mediately picked up on my irregular stride. Just like people, dogs have vary-ing tolerances for pain. Often, our instinct is to suffer in silence so as not to appear weak. Not me, though. Limping like Chester on *Gunsmoke*, I want the sympathy vote.

There are lots of ways a dog can tell you he's in pain. It could be vocal, behavioral, postural, or simply by appearance. Any change in your pup's usual way of acting or moving could signify pain.

If my limp doesn't disappear soon, I'll be visiting the vet to be sure it's nothing serious. In the meantime, I'm enjoying lounging and watching lots of DVDs.

Love,

Lady

Memories Are Made of This . . .

Dear Diary,

You know, dogs do have a memory.

Diane Sawyer even said so on *CBS News*.

She interviewed a border collie named Chaser whose vocabulary numbered a whole thousand words. (I wonder if mozzarella is one of them?) Chaser's owner and trainer is an astrophysicist. Jeanne is, well, not an astrophysicist. In fact, she admits to difficulty even spelling the word. See where I'm going with this?

I'm really not sure how many words I know. I can't count, so how would I be able to tell? But I am sure that I have a good memory. Can we take a stroll down Memory Lane so I can prove it? Here are some highlights of the ten weeks I've spent with this pack:

Day 1 gave way to total sensory overload as I was confronted with indoor life after two years in an outdoor pen. I had never before heard the washer and dryer spinning, microwave beeping, hairdryer screaming, or telephone ringing. On Day 5, I learned how to run beside Jeanne riding her bike.

The divine Miss Rayne, age almost-three, was formally introduced to me on Day 8. I instantly loved her somethin' wicked, even though she told me I have eye boogies. The Bark Park visit, together with my first fan mail, summed up Day 11. I learned a huge lesson on Day 12—THE LOOK. Avoid it at all costs. It could turn you into a stone garden ornament. Poof!

I partied hearty on Day 17 at my first dinner engagement. Way cool. I was introduced to the beach on Day 19 and was enthralled by the sand, salt water, and ocean breeze.

I went to a ladies' golf party on Day 24 to practice walking through a crowd. Was I ever a big hit with those super friendly gals! On Day 25 I talked about my foster brother, Joe, alias Mr. Wonderful.

I played my first nine holes on the golf links on Day 31. Love that cart. Went boating on Day 33 and discovered that I was born for this. The pack went on full alert on Day 39 when the AKC Good Citizen test was scheduled. A few days later, Jeanne asked me to consider taking the Therapy Dog test in addition to the AKCGC. I'm a golden, so we all know what the answer was.

Day 45 found me lean but not mean. I'd lost five-and-a-half pounds since joining up with this pack. Can you believe that, after all this time, Day 47 was my first shopping visit to Walmart? I marched directly to the cheese aisle and picked out two pounds of mozzarella.

A *huge* day for my pack was Day 50, when I proudly reported that we passed both the AKC Good Citizen and Therapy Dog tests. We rested on our laurels for about eleven minutes and then proceeded to the next phase of my service dog training. Phew.

Since the first time I jumped into Lulu and joined this pack, it has been one exhilarating, wonderful ride! Dean Martin sings it swell: "Sweet, sweet the memories you gave-a me. Can't beat, the memories you gave-a me."

Love,

Lady

A Letter to My Mom

**Lady tells Jeanne, "I trust you
with my life."**

Dear Mom,

To be miserable, you don't need practice. So I must not dwell on the morning when I will wake up without you and Bode beside me.

I've been asked countless times, "How could you possibly leave Jeanne?"

The answer is, "I don't know."

You are my foster mother, and I will be forever honored by your willingness to bring me into your pack. Your love, affection, training skills, and generosity have touched me to my core.

So I don't know how I can give you up, but I know that I will, and I know that I will find comfort in helping make life a little easier for a deserving veteran. I will work relentlessly to make you and Bode proud.

On the day when I look away from you and move toward my adopting veteran—easily, willingly, happily—I hope you will see it as my tribute to you.

When you turn over that Tupperware container of the mozzarella I love so much, my veteran will have been taught everything about me: where to scratch, when to reward, when a sharp correction is in order, and how to Dremel my nails and comb my gorgeous locks. And should questions arise, he or she will have all manner of phone, cell, and email contacts to use at any hour of day or night.

I hope you find comfort in the fact that I will adjust to my new life quickly and seamlessly . . . thanks to you.

Love always,

Your Golden Girl

P.S. I write this now—not because my departure is imminent—but because when that day does come, I may not be up to writing.

A Fashion Statement

Dear Diary,

Please don't think I've gone all highfalutin', but I do have some fashion advice for your consideration. Chic it isn't; functional it is! It's one of the best gifts I've ever given Jeanne. She wears it every day.

I'm referring to her fishing vest. Of course, in this pack we wouldn't know a rod from a reel, but we ladies do know our sportswear, and this cute little accessory makes even the hastiest exits from the house go smoothly.

It's made mostly of mesh netting, so it's cool to wear even in the hottest weather. It has eighteen pockets, all of which have zippered or Velcro closures. Eighteen! That means Jeanne has dedicated pockets for: my treats, Bode's hypoallergenic treats, poop bags, house and car keys, cell phone, camera, fetch ball, sunglasses, tissues, sunblock, bug repellant, and anything else Bode and I might need. Everything is pre-stocked and replenished as necessary.

No longer are Bode and I waiting impatiently at the garage door while Jeanne interrogates herself, "Do I have my phone, enough poop bags?" When she takes that vest off the hook by the door, we are outta here in a flash.

Another plus: no more pants pockets ruined by greasy treats. No more searching for an outfit that has the most pockets before we can head to the beach.

I do admit that this vest may never sport the label of a celebrity fashionista. You might not want to wear it on a date, and some have even called it "granola." But it wins the functionality factor, paws down!

Love,

Lady

A Funny Thing Happened

Dear Diary,

A funny thing happened on our way through the laundry room. As we passed the washer and dryer, a light went on (in Jeanne's head). She thought back to an advertisement picturing service dogs removing clothes from a dryer. So she decided we could do that taking-the-clothes-out-of-the-dryer thing.

And the training began.

Often our modus operandi is that Bode learns the task first while I sit and watch. Then it's my turn to copycat him. This was no different. The first thing he extracted from the dryer was several cubes of mozzarella. By now I'm drooling, "Send me in, coach. Send me in; I can do cheese!" But, no.

Then the cheese was replaced with our favorite ball. "Bring ball, Bode." No sweat. He brought the ball and we both got a modest treat (Milk-Bone Minis, five calories each). I should interject here that whenever either one of us does something good, we *both* get a reward. It's a team spirit sort of thing so that we always root for each other.

The next object to hit the dryer was a boring old clean dishtowel. Who could want that? Bode took a stab at it, then turned around and fixed Jeanne with an imploring stare. "Mom, are you sure you want this stupid rag?" I'm with him. Lose the dishtowel.

Training is often about obligingly doing the things you don't want to do, not the stuff that comes easily. I'm told there will be a gently used dishtowel at tomorrow's training session. That'll smell a little more interesting than the clean one.

Love,

Lady

Bode demonstrates how to remove items from the dryer.

Missed Kodak Moments

Dear Diary,

We should have an in-house photographer to capture some of the amazingly funny, amazingly joyful, amazingly adorable happenings Bode and I are into around here.

Usually Jeanne can be found somewhere on the perimeter. She knows that if she moves so much as a muscle to get the camera, that photo op will be gone forever. I'll try to describe some of the moments you might have enjoyed, had we captured them on film:

- Me, doing my bear hug imitation while trying to climb up a tree trunk to reach a squirrel;
- Me, tenderly licking Bode's annoyed face all over like our mothers used to do;
- Me, trying with all my might to levitate up to the sky to catch a bird;
- Me, putting my head and shoulders under Bode's belly, then standing up and tipping him over;
- Bode and me, sleeping head to head diagonally across the bed;
- Me, when the light in my eyes shines like liquid gold;
- Bode and me, napping so close together that our feathers overlap, and the only way to tell us apart is by the color of our collars;
- Me, galloping through the ocean surf with wild abandon; and
- Me, curious, tilting my head at a flirtatious angle—or like right now, resting it companionably against Jeanne's leg while she types.

Even without these images immortalized in photos, I know I am indelibly imprinted in Jeanne's heart and Bode's—and, I hope, yours.

Love,

Lady

Could He Be My Veteran?

Gordon and Lady get acquainted.

Dear Diary,

Jeanne took me to meet a veteran today. I like him. He smells good. And he likes me.

He's a little older than I am, but dogs don't care about age.

We have lots of stuff in common. We both like golf. He likes to travel in his RV, and I love to ride. He likes to talk, and I enjoy listening.

He has a nice house with a good backyard, and his living room couch is comfortable. I've heard that the media room couch is even softer but haven't tried out that one yet. He has a confident-sounding voice that relaxes me. Plus, he has grandchildren who live somewhere at the end of an RV trip. I know I'll love that.

I'm thinking we could be a team.

Gordon is a disabled Vietnam veteran, but that makes no difference to me. Dogs don't care at all about disabilities. Clearly, his life could be enriched by the comfort, companionship, and tasks a service dog could provide. And I think that dog could be me.

Up-close and personal exposure to thundering artillery fire during army service left Gordon severely hearing impaired. I could learn to alert him to important sounds like phones ringing, doorbells buzzing, smoke alarms beeping, or car horns blasting.

So, it looks like we plan to "take things to the next level." The plan is something about gradually transitioning me and seeing if everything works for everyone.

I heard that Gordon bought some mozzarella to have on hand when I come for my next visit. Did I mention that he is also smart?

Love,

Lady

Matching a Service Dog with a Partner

Dear Diary,

Many adoptees never know the details of their earlier lives, nor do they know how they came to live in a new home. I am luckier than most. Jeanne keeps better records than the IRS, and every major detail of my life as her foster dog is catalogued, including photos, in my "baby album."

One interesting letter in it was written by the Canine Angels boss (Rick) after our first meeting with Gordon (my prospective veteran). It explains the initial steps toward matching a service dog with a potential life partner. Here's how it goes . . .

Canine Angels President Rick Kaplan
hugs one of his favorite girls.

Hi Gordon,

Thanks for having us in your home today. We all felt welcome and comfortable.

Jeanne and I were thrilled about Lady's reaction to you. Her body language clearly indicated a comfort level and trust in you that translated into an immediate desire to be close to you. This is not by any means her usual reaction, since she is generally shy and reserved. There is just no explaining things to a dog, so we could not prepare her for what is polite, or what we hoped for. That is what makes a dog's affection so valuable. There is no forewarning, no acting, no pretense. What the dog feels and how the dog acts thereafter is real and undeniable.

What we need from you is the same level of candidness that we got from Lady with regard to your inner sense and emotions. Did you like her, did you feel any connection to her, and did your heart tell you that you could share your life with her? Did you feel the unique and extraordinary character within her? We urge you to reply with absolute honesty, no matter what the answer is, since there is no point in trying to build a skyscraper on a weak foundation. If it is yes, we will start planning to proceed immediately. If it is no, we will continue our search for the right pup for you . . .

Rick, Jeanne, and Lady

Gordon Is Smitten

Dear Diary,

Jeanne says that I have cast my spell. My veteran, Gordon, seems smitten with me. He thinks I'm beautiful. Here's his take on our first meeting.

Love,

Lady

Dear Rick,

I enjoyed having you, Jeanne, and the pack visit yesterday. I was pleased with Lady and think she would make an excellent companion for me. She is a beautiful dog, and the fact that she is already a golf lover is a definite plus. I was also thinking that my grandchildren would undoubtedly like Lady, which is an important consideration for me as well. I was even pondering your question as to whether I would be willing to have a service dog sleep on my bed, knowing full well that those kinds of decisions tend to be irreversible when it comes to dogs. I can see that Lady already feels that she has squatter's rights to my living room couch. However, she may change her mind when she discovers the couch in the media room.

Since I have had no previous experience with her, I will trust your judgment as to Lady's reaction to me. While I did sense that we were bonding, I also sensed that her apparent interest in me was tempered to some degree by her loyalty to Jeanne, which is to be expected.

The thought of being an ambassador to the program that goes along with Lady is truly inviting. So I am ready to proceed as soon as you and Jeanne are.

Gordon

Learning on the Links

St. James Golf Plantation treats Lady royally.

Dear Diary,

Today was fun. I rode eighteen holes in the golf cart with my prospective new partner, Gordon. I'm pretty sure he's a keeper. He brought treats and mozzarella, plus ice cubes to keep my water bowl full and cool.

Best of all, he talked to me all the way around the golf course. He explained what he wanted to happen, what might happen, and what actually did happen. I guess that was thanks to his military training. I'm pretty sure he was happiest when what he wanted to happen matched up with what actually did happen.

The few times I took a misstep, he was understanding and supportive. You just don't morph from chain-link-fence dog to golf course diva without a hiccup or two. Gordon obviously understood this.

I think he was proud of me because he introduced me to everyone—from golf professional Steve, to the assistant pro intern Nick, bag boys Jay and John, several restaurant patrons, and even John the bartender. It was hot out there, readers, so after playing they sat down to enjoy a frosty cool one while I lay at their feet reveling in the AC.

Many thanks to Steve Elkington, the club pro at Player's Course–St. James Plantation, because he made it a point to meet me and allowed Jeanne and me to play for free since we were there on Gordon's behalf. Everyone on the staff of St. James was wonderfully welcoming. Great place!

Love,

Lady

A Family Vacation without Me?

Dear Diary,

Imagine my surprise when she packed the suitcase without including so much as a cotton ball belonging to me or Bode. Hmmph!

Jeanne was about to make a solo trip to California to visit some of our family whom she hadn't seen in a while—Emily, Jason, and Joseph. Then the pet sitter came to look after Bode, and I was transferred temporarily to the super-sized Canine Angels pack for advanced training.

Although I missed Jeanne ever so much and was somewhat unsure of my place among all those other dogs, I did try hard to adjust. But I soon became less than happy when I was confronted with the advanced requirements I would have to master to qualify as a service dog. The constant demands and expectations of instant obedience were overwhelming, so I decided to quit performing. I literally lay down and waited for Jeanne to come get me . . . like she did once before.

Love,
Lady

Sticking with My Instincts

Dear Diary,

My journey to become a service dog has officially ended.

Rather than sadness, this is cause for celebration because I have a new job—as a therapy dog. To help you understand the process, I'm sharing with you another letter from the boss:

Dear Readers,

Lady has been a success from the moment of her rescue, for we knew without a doubt that, at the very least, we would basic-train her, socialize her, and find her a loving and forever home. We did that. Jeanne broke all barriers by taking her to amazing heights in record time. After only two months of training, Lady passed the AKC Canine Good Citizen and Therapy Dogs International tests. She was an eager, willing, and hungry student all the way. Through her instinctive determination, this dog was attempting to be all that she could be.

So, while Jeanne visited her kids in California one week, I took Lady into the main pack for advanced training. It soon became apparent that service dog status would not be the best path for her. This was made absolutely clear to me through her reactions to the elevated level of training. I attempted many different approaches over several days, and each time Lady reinforced the same message: "I am happy where I am. I know I can do the most good as a therapy dog."

My difficult choice was to consider the possibility of trying to force the service dog issue, which might damage or destroy the advanced accomplishments she had already achieved. I chose, therefore, not to proceed.

Lady will remain a certified Canine Angels Therapy Dog, and her journey to become a service dog has officially ended. She has attained a different goal, not a lesser goal.

From the beginning, Jeanne had the option to keep her foster charge if she ever felt that she could not part with this dog. Despite her emotional connection with Lady, often expressed in her daily reports called Lady Grams, she pressed on toward our stated goal of making Lady a working service dog for a disabled American veteran. Her singular purpose was to get to that finish line, regardless of personal attachment.

The situation at hand now, however, is not about the human but about the dog, who is always our first consideration. I have asked Jeanne to adopt Lady and make her part of her therapy team. On this path, Lady will bring smiles, laughter, and joy to hundreds, if not thousands, of veterans and others for the rest of her working life.

This decision is all about Lady because I feel without a doubt that her place in Jeanne's permanent pack is her destiny. After much reflection, Jeanne also believes that this is the inevitable solution for Lady, and for all.

Many of you will be thrilled about this turn of events; others may question whether this is some sort of failure. I can assure you that Lady's story is an absolute success in every way. Her bright future will bear this out. We at Canine Angels have a series of possible goals, any one of which reached is cause for celebration. I hope you will all celebrate this one with us.

A note about Gordon, the veteran with whom we had hoped to pair Lady: Gordon understood and graciously accepted Lady's new future, despite his disappointment. This has been a valuable learning experience for all concerned, which will surely make us better at our respective roles in an often complex process. (Gordon has since been successfully paired with Major, a Canine Angels service dog who continues to serve him.)

Rick Kaplan, Founder and President of Canine Angels, Inc.

My GPS Maps a New Route

**A pensive expression comes over
Lady as she considers a new path.**

Dear Diary,

I have sorely missed writing to you. So much has been happening in my life, and I want to update everyone.

My internal GPS recently led me onto a road less traveled by other Canine Angels. At first I was nervous about the change in direction, but now I am relieved, relaxed, and eager to hit the road running. My new journey will be as a therapy dog, not as a service dog.

I have already attained my therapy credentials and made some practice visits, so I am anxious to pursue this new path. Jeanne says I have a natural gift for bringing smiles to people in hospice care, nursing homes, schools, and adult day care and substance abuse care centers. Bringing smiles is a therapy dog's main job.

I told Jeanne and Rick last week that I wanted to switch my major from service to therapy. Students switch majors all the time. I told them with every ounce of body language I could muster that the advanced training was traumatic for me. I simply shut down and fought against complying. They got my message and eventually agreed that service work is not where I can "be all that I can be."

I am going where my strengths lie and where my heart lies—in therapy work. Service and therapy are both noble endeavors, just different. I overheard Jeanne and Rick say, "Why take a violin virtuoso and make her a pianist? Let her use her unique talents for her own well-being and for the good of the many who can benefit by all that she has to offer."

My almost-partner, Gordon, will continue to work with Canine Angels to find a new dog who will qualify to perform hearing assistance tasks for him. We like him a lot and hope to hang out with him on occasion. He is a good man.

Some dogs are destined to serve one master, and others can help many. Therapy is the best route my GPS could ever have imagined. And, it allows me to remain at home with my forever pack, Jeanne and Bode—the two who make me smile every day.

There will be no purple service dog vest in my wardrobe, and no guaranteed entry to restaurants, stores, planes, or golf courses. But now I belong to a pack that I will forever love and cherish. I have a mom, a brother, a great home, and Lulu to take me to the beach every day. What more could a girl want?

As most of you know, the dust almost never settles around here—like those laurels we never get to rest on. I will continue to learn more skills, meet more people, and visit more places to make more therapy visits. "More" is always as good as it gets. I'll keep you posted.

Love,

Lady

Change Is in the Air

Dear Diary,

Things are a bit different around here now. I mean, since I became a permanent pack member. Don't worry—it's different in a good way. I can see, hear, and smell that something has changed, and I think I know what it is.

When I switched from service to therapy dog, Jeanne and Bode automatically erased the line they had subconsciously drawn to separate foster from family.

I believe that each had blocked off a tiny piece of heart to keep from loving me too much. They did this to prepare for the likelihood that I would break their hearts when I left. They needed that little piece to remain unbroken to help them heal.

It's self-preservation, a predictable human emotion. I can understand this, even though I'm a dog. You see, I'm a therapy dog, so we get it. I'm happy to say that now my new status allows them to love me completely, unconditionally, and forever—as I do them.

Love,
Lady

Mending Fences

**Bode, Lady, and Catcher listen to the
rules for peaceful coexistence.**

Dear Diary,

Most of you have already heard of Catcher, the Chesapeake Bay retriever who lives next door to my pack. Did you know that, up to today, I'd thought that Catcher didn't like me?

Hey, I was not about to lose any sleep over it. Maybe I reminded her of an unpleasant someone from her past. Maybe I smelled weird to her. Maybe she was miffed that I'm prettier than she is (meow). No big deal. Not everyone has to like everyone else.

Jeanne, on the other hand, *did* lose sleep over it. First, there were a couple incidents of aggression which, I am told, were unLadylike. My position was: "Honestly, *she* was the one who started it." This paw pointing prompted a discussion about both of us being at fault. Then Catcher was banished from pack road trips because any shenanigans inside Lulu could be hazardous to our health.

This meant that she would miss out on lots of fun: No beach walks, no swims in the Intracoastal Waterway, no strolls through the wooded paths at Vereen Gardens, not even a ride to Walmart.

So we decided to mend that fence. Jeanne hatched a plan for introducing, reinforcing, and maintaining peaceful coexistence between Catcher and me. Could she have chosen a hotter evening for the first training session? At six o'clock p.m. it was still about ninety-five—hot enough to make even the most benevolent dog ill-tempered. But we persevered, making giant leaps of progress irrigated by giant ponds of perspiration.

As usual, we began with carefully supervised baby steps, sitting side by side on leash, ultimately venturing a furtive sniff and wisely avoiding eye contact.

It turns out that Catcher has no instinctual dislike of me. There are just a few situations when she wants me to stay out of her face. Vehemently. One instance is when I try to get my head out "her" window on car rides. So Jeanne commissioned a nice comfy flat area on Lulu's front passenger seat. Catcher will ride there, always on leash. I tested out this area when Catcher wasn't looking. I thought it was swell, but I'm really glad that Bode and I will have the whole back seat to ourselves.

So, guess where we were at six a.m. today? Sitting in Catcher's driveway in Lulu while Jeanne went to retrieve her (get it?). Then Catcher hopped into her cute little space in the front, deftly opened the treat compartment, snuck a few Minis, and slurped a bit of Jeanne's coffee. Then off we sped to the beach. Everyone was civilized.

When we pulled into the parking lot, Catcher squealed with joy. We couldn't wait to hit the sand and waves. Three big dogs parading down the beach on leashes (all held by one apparent lightweight) was a sight to see. Predictably, my softy mom had tears in her eyes to see me and Catcher trotting happily side by side.

We were let off leash one at a time. If we girls, all wound up with excitement, had been turned loose simultaneously, it could have pushed one of us over the edge. So for now we'll be closely controlled.

I used my off-leash time wisely, running full tilt through the surf to race a bunch of birds but never coming close enough to catch one. When I returned, Catcher went free. The girl is *fast*. She ran back and forth, back and forth in knee-deep water, just for the sheer joy of it. It was a sight to behold. Bode used his free time to troll around the trash barrels, just in case an errant toss had left some food on the sand.

We girls asked him how he could ignore the most beautiful beach in the world in favor of a few dirty old trash cans. Although he knew it was a rhetorical question, he responded: "Different dogs dig different treasures."

Love,

Lady

Cabana Guys

Dear Diary,

July has just begun, and it's already the dog days of summer. Eighty-one degrees as we drove to the beach at five forty-five this morning. Whew!

We have company—again. I'm told that when you live near the beach in the summer, your popularity soars with the ocean breeze. So I've been entertaining Hunter, a sixteen-month-old golden-haired shih tzu who's about ten pounds of huggable.

Bode and I call him "The Little Emperor" behind his back because he's always trying to boss us around. That's pretty cheeky for a guy who's one-fifth my size. Jeanne said he's "intact," which might be what makes him act macho. What's "macho"? For that matter, what's "intact"? I don't think it's contagious, so I'm not worried, but it seems that maybe he'd be better off "unintact."

Anticipating Hunter's arrival, we relocated our usual walk to a different stretch of the beach. It's a bit less crowded, which is better for Hunter since he knows *nada* about beach etiquette. (Check out my Spanish!) Clearly, the change of location had nothing to do with the fact that several cute young college guys are at this end of the beach every day setting up cabanas. Jeanne swears to this.

The guys usually arrive just as our pack is leaving the beach. On the first day we were told "no visit" and had to walk past them directly to the boardwalk. The workers watched with one eye on us and the other on their work. There was good energy in the air. I could smell the potential for unbridled fun.

Day Two: The guys called greetings to us, so Jeanne allowed us to "go say hello." Five minutes of bedlam ensued. Bode hugged and licked them. Hunter jumped on everyone. (He has since been made to practice "Off!") I girlishly wiggled and wagged my way over to each guy.

Day Three: We pups started galloping down the beach the moment we caught the cabana guys' scents. They glanced up from their work just in time to brace themselves for our gleeful charge. I ran at them full throttle and flopped unceremoniously at their feet—legs splayed, tail thrashing, head bobbing, grinning ear to ear. Totally delighted, they grinned back at me.

These joyful daily greetings have been going on all week. This morning one of the guys held my face in his hands as we were getting ready to leave. He looked into my eyes and told me, "You make my day."

Love,

Lady

Sharing Memories

Dear Diary,

This week my pack is in remembrance mode. It's not a national holiday or anything. It's partly due to the 9-11 anniversary. Bode and I weren't alive then, but Jeanne has told us about that horrific attack and the heroes who surfaced as first responders. I heard that some of them were canines.

Today our memories are also brought on by an annual charity golf tournament whose proceeds go toward preventing and curing cancer. We buy special pink flags "in honor of" or "in memory of" loved ones who have survived or succumbed to cancer. A different kind of horror.

One of the most special loved ones in our memory is Casey Maxon, the first golden retriever in Jeanne's pack. He died of cancer six years ago, at age eight. Jeanne still talks a lot about "my Casey Max," and from the stories I've heard her tell, I know I would have loved him. Bode would have too.

Casey would ride all over the plantation with his head sticking out the car sunroof and his jowls flapping in the wind. People would laugh and wave to him. One time he jumped into a huge mud puddle, then ran into the neighbor's house through a closed screen door, and landed on the white satin comforter that covered their bed. After that incident, Jeanne thought she'd have to move, but everyone forgave Casey for just about anything.

His irresistible face graced the cover of every family Christmas card sent in his lifetime. When he was unhappy about riding in the new car, they had a sunroof installed for him. Most of the golfers knew him well, because he would often sneak over to the Lion's Paw 10th green to help them putt. He could never hear the sound of people laughing on their back decks without considering this an invitation to join them for an hors d'oeuvre or two.

Bode and I share many of Casey's traits, and we, too, are loved beyond belief. It's a good feeling to know that we, too, will always be remembered. Like the legend of the Rainbow Bridge, the pink flags in Casey's memory signify that, while he is gone from our lives, he will never be absent from our hearts.

Love,

Lady

**Casey Maxon considered every laugh
an invitation to visit.**

First Day of School

**Bode and Lady are ready to
strut their therapy dog stuff.**

Dear Diary,

Now that the kids are back in school, my first visit was scheduled for today. After enjoying a peaceful summer full of running and playing, I was raring to get to work. It was time to strut my stuff as a therapy dog.

I was excited and a little nervous. Jeanne said it was okay to have butterflies in my stomach, as long as I made them fly in formation. I thought we'd just roll out of bed, load up into Lulu, and hit the road. No way.

We had to prepare for school the same way the kids do: wake up, potty break, nutritious breakfast, practice our lessons, and some morning exercise. Of course, we couldn't leave the house without a thorough beauty parlor treatment: teeth brushed, ears cleaned, toenails filed, and coat brushed to a shine. Jeanne also issued some reminders about polite behavior.

The purpose of this first visit was to attend a new volunteers orientation meeting. I thought that sounded like something requiring a leather briefcase, but Jeanne shot down that idea pretty quick. And I would have seriously loved a ride on the big yellow school bus with the flashing lights. Request denied.

When we arrived at the school, our friend Ronna was Bode's handler, and Jeanne watched over me. Bode led the way, touring us down the second-grade corridor and then on to the meeting room. Then he and I lay on the purple Pilates mat and listened to a few briefings. I didn't get to sniff any kids yet, but I did meet the principal. She smelled nice. When she spoke, she made me wish I could read.

Bode shared small bits of "insider information" with me from his two years of listening to second graders read. He knew all the teachers and their classrooms. He did advise me that, when in Miss Mill's class, I really must toe the line. If the students got a little wired and she yelled, "Eyes on Miss Mill!" my eyes had better be among those trained on hers. She meant business. Even Jeanne does "eyes on Miss Mill!"

For sure, having Bode's example to follow will make it easier for me. But we do have different personalities, mine being a little reserved and polite, compared to his exuberant friendliness. I know I will soon have fans of my own. I look forward to this and to sharing with you some new stories about our work.

Love,

Lady

Birthday Behests

Dear Diary,

With Bode's birthday coming up I've overheard some talk about gifts and celebrations. I know for sure that we'll have our delicious peanut butter Frosty Paws ice cream cups. That's a given. I doubt that we'll have pony rides, clowns, or party hats.

Bode wanted to register for gifts from the pet treat aisle at Walmart, but that got shot down. It seems that our pack leader doesn't believe in such practices. I know what I'd like to give Bode. I'd arrange for him to sit beside the Walmart greeter for an entire morning and get patted by all who enter. He's such an attention hog! Add a few treats to the mix and he'd be in seventh (or maybe even eighth) heaven.

My birthday is in late December. I'm going to be three, and I've never had a birthday party before. If I do have one, it might get lumped in with the holidays and then get overshadowed by Christmas. So Bode has advised me to write up my birthday wish list early—before the season kicks off and they start stringing popcorn and hanging up mistletoe. (I wonder what "mistletoe" is—something to do with your feet?)

Not sure where I could register for everything I want, even if registering was allowed in this pack. But here's my list anyway. I would like:

- Slower and lower flying birds at the beach;
- Less "leave it" and more "take it" commands;
- Mozzarella—tons of mozzarella;
- A moratorium on THE LOOK;

- To catch just one squirrel in my yard (and then let it go unscathed for next time);
- Permission to eat the rest of the squeaky toy after removing the squeaker;
- Frozen peanut butter KONGs—lots of them;
- A moratorium on the "away" command;
- To have Catcher admit she likes me;
- To be fed first—*every* single time;
- Serial ear scratching—at any hour of the day or night;
- More hard-boiled eggs and carrots;
- Toenails that don't grow and need to be Dremeled; and
- A front seat ride in a convertible with the top down, of course.

I am also thinking about the bigger picture. "It's not always about you two," Bode and I have been told. There are several other things that I wish for. But we can't just *wish*. We have to *work* for: cures for canine cancer and other illnesses; universal no-kill shelters; and unanimously responsible pet owners.

Last but not least, I wish and work for the continued success of each and every entity that helps rescue and place homeless dogs.

Love,

Lady

Costumed for Halloween

Dear Diary,

You know those silly emails lots of dog lovers receive around Halloween with the subject line, "Why Dogs Hate Their Owners"? Usually a bunch of embarrassing photos of pups all gussied up in outrageous costumes. Sometimes they're funny; they're often foolish and thought by many to be humiliating for dogs.

Not mine. I totally *loved* my outfit that I wore to the adult day care center today. I was a surfer girl, and was I ever stylin' in a formfitting pink spandex body suit. I must say, I looked really *fine*. Felt so fine, it made me prance.

Some effort was wasted in attempting to affix a matching pink headband over my ears, but that got pawed off and chewed up in seconds and never made it out of the car. No sense being *gauche*, I thought. Like my French?

My friend, Ronna, got my costume at a yard sale. Bode got one too, but being a guy, he isn't much interested in wardrobe unless it smells stinky or is edible. No luck, Bode.

We thought the costumes would help make the daycare people smile, and we were right.

Love,
Lady

A Passion for Running

**Lady and Bode return to Jeanne
after a dash through the surf.**

Dear Diary,

Running is my passion. Running *fast*.

Add knee-deep ocean waves backed by the rising sun and a flight of star-tled birds just out of reach—and I'm euphoric.

I discovered this passion some months ago when our pack began beach walking each morning. In one short week I progressed from fearing the ti-niest wave touching my toes to swimming in water so deep that it's over my head. One day I began running endlessly back and forth through the surf, parallel to the shore. At times I found birds to chase; at other times not.

Jeanne says I am faster than a speeding bullet. I think that reference comes from an old radio show about some guy who can fly and goes around wearing tights and a cape. Who knows where she gets these ideas. Sometimes she puts me on leash to rest for a bit out of concern for my heart. There wasn't any running room to speak of in my old chain-link pen, so I wasn't sufficiently conditioned when this passion first presented itself.

No one taught me to run. It just happened. Certainly Bode, a.k.a. Couch Potato, did not set the example. And goldens really aren't noted for speed. But *I* am an exception.

One of the great things about this passion is that it fits nicely into my job as a therapy dog. You know—the part about how I'm supposed to make people smile? Every day people stop to watch me run. They say things like: "Pure joy! What fun! She's having a ball!" And as they watch, they smile.

Just doin' my job.

Love,

Lady

Fall Foliage Fun

Dear Diary,

Brrr! New Hampshire is cold! I found that out on my first-ever pack vacation when we drove up to the Granite State this past week.

On my first morning there, I was sent out to do my business in twenty-three-degree weather and practically froze my ears off. When we went out later on, I ran and ran and never got hot due to inhaling the frigid air. I think I like the cold.

On the next morning we woke up to find a ten-inch blanket of the most amazing fluffy white stuff covering the yard, and I met snow for the first time in my life. With the snow came all sorts of new games—chasing snowballs, lying on my back to carve snow angels, and leaping joyfully through the drifts like a gazelle. (A "gazelle"?) Thoroughly awesome!

This trip taught me a bunch of new words like: "nor'easter," "foliage," and "E-ZPass." A storm like the nor'easter that dumped all that wonderful snow before Halloween apparently hadn't happened there since the Civil War, whenever and whatever that was. Many people were surprised, including us.

We hiked into the White Mountains on three different trails, all decked out with a stunning display of foliage. We swam under waterfalls and waded in rushing streams of crystal-clear cold water. I really couldn't see how vibrant the leaves were because dogs can only distinguish certain shades of color. But when I heard Jeanne describe it, I knew the autumn hue must have been spectacular. Auntie Janet made bright orange vests for Bode and me because it was hunting season and they didn't want us to be mistaken for deer.

Night skies in New Hampshire have the twinkliest stars imaginable. I was wishing we had the Constellation App for the iPhone to identify them. I guess we'd also need an iPhone.

When you walk on the frozen snow, it makes the nicest crunchy sound under your feet, sort of like when you chomp on a big crusty dog bone.

Bode and I were assigned copilot duties on the 2,131 miles we drove Lulu. That included ten states and quite a few tollbooths. I must have stuck my head out the window to greet at least a dozen toll takers, and they all had a friendly word or two for me. One even had dog cookies! (She's on the New Jersey Turnpike, in case you're headed that way.)

Unfortunately, Bode got distracted from his duties and let Jeanne drive through the E-ZPass lane, twice. And we don't have an E-ZPass! Jeanne told us to smile for the cameras that would probably photograph us in the act of sneaking through without paying. If we get a ticket, I refuse to be held responsible. It will just have to come out of Bode's allowance.

I slept at three different houses and met six new dogs, two cats, and a parakeet, plus lots of new people. My thank-you note list includes: Penny and Bo (cocker spaniels), Delia and Dugan (cats who stayed on top of the fridge for our entire visit), Kenzie (yellow lab puppy), Belle (Rottweiler mixer), Butch (Chihuahua), Scooby (Scottish terrier), and Tweety the bird.

I took everything in stride and was a terrific houseguest, if I do say so. When we got home and jumped out of Lulu, I was surprised to be greeted by North Carolina's balmy seventy degrees. I guess I have a lot to learn about latitudes. Oy vey, more vocabulary.

From rescued dog to delighted vacationer? Imagine that!

Where to next? I'm up for anyplace, but I hope Santa brings Lulu an E-ZPass.

Love,

Lady

Lady luxuriates in the icy waters.

Life at the Goldens' B&B

Ever the gracious hostess, Lady shares her pillow with Abby.

Dear Diary,

We've temporarily increased our pack to four. Abby, the cutie-pie white terrier mix from the super-sized pack, has joined us for a week's vacation. She told me her invitation to the out-of-town wedding that Rick was attending must have been lost in the mail. Anyway, we're happy to have her visit.

Abby arrived here last night, just in time for supper. Jeanne told her she would be dining *al fresco*, which must mean in the bathroom, so she could eat in peace without Bode and I waiting to pounce on her food dish. She's a slower eater than we are. Who isn't? We were waiting outside the bathroom door for ten minutes before she emerged with the empty dish in her mouth. Nice to know that she, too, has to clear away her plate.

We took a walk down our street so the neighbors could ask themselves, "Who's the new kid in that pack?" We wanted them to know where Abby belonged in case she wandered off and couldn't find her way back.

Afterward, we played a little ball, then came in and watched Abby remove the countless bones, KONGs, and balls from our toy box and litter the kitchen floor with them. She sure likes to make a mess. Other than that, she seems to have nice manners.

We eventually settled in to fall asleep in front of the television. Apparently, Abby snores. At least Jeanne says so. I can't be sure because it wasn't so loud as to keep me awake. I understand it was a ladylike snore. Most of all, I was happy that Abby didn't hog too much space on our bed. She picked a spot at the foot, curled up into a ball, and hardly moved until the crack of dawn. Actually, when we wake up, dawn hasn't even cracked yet.

After a quick walk, we were ready for breakfast. Abby dined al fresco again, but this time with the bathroom door open. She'll soon be dining side by side with Bode and me.

Finally, it was time to load up into Lulu and head to the beach for our morning ritual. Abby was allowed to ride shotgun, which got my knickers in a twist, but I don't think it was favoritism. We were just making sure everybody had their own window.

I noticed that Abby was *way* impressed with our beach. Bode and I were *way* impressed with Abby. She runs faster than a rocket (I'm the only speeding bullet) and more powerfully than a locomotive. But we really must teach her to veer off before crashing into us at top speed.

She didn't go far into the water, but that will probably change. I know about this routine because I didn't dare to try to swim when I first met the beach six months ago. Jeanne and Bode helped me learn. I'll help Abby.

Love,

Lady

I Want My Three-Pack Back

Dear Diary,

If I were a drinking girl, I would chugalug a tall glass of whiskey, put my paws up on the ottoman, and pass out.

I just survived a morning from hell.

During our routine exercise regimen that starts in the darkness before sunrise at the beach, Bode suddenly went missing. He had been following behind us, as is his custom, and the next time we looked back, he had vanished.

Mom and I and lots of our great friends searched for nearly three hours. We combed through the brush-covered dunes, patrolled all the wooden walkways to the beach, and cruised the roads—calling, calling, calling his name. Nothing.

We alerted the police. My aunts drove an hour to our home to be there in case he made his way back while we were searching. Our other family members who live too far away were stationed by their cell phones waiting for word. Someone trained binoculars on the dunes from the third-floor deck of a beach house. Complete strangers volunteered to help look.

I saw Mom crying, but I pretended not to notice. I just stuck with her the whole time and helped in the only way I know how, by being with her. I was afraid that she was beginning to lose the battle against panic.

After covering many more miles, we walked out of the dunes and onto the beach again for at least the tenth time, terribly scared and dejected. Then we looked north up the beach and saw a small dot moving along, possibly a quarter of a mile away. The dot soon turned golden in color and seemed to break into a gallop toward us over the sand, soaking wet and smiling.

Mom didn't even ask him where he'd been. She just went down on her knees and laid her face against his dripping coat. And after all was said and done, he was *so* on her S-list. Bode, you got some 'splainin' to do.

Love,

Lady

Responding to a Scare

Dear Diary,

When one of us canines makes a mistake around here, oftentimes we *both* have to pay. And, on occasion, the pack leader has been known to over-react. Just sayin'.

Last week Bode went missing at the beach for three hours, so guess how *innocent I* have spent my days since then.

First, neither of us got to go to the beach for three days because Jeanne said she was now gun shy—whatever that is. I don't know anything about guns, but I know I can be a little shy at times. No need to stay home over it.

When we finally did venture out, Bode had to be on leash at all times, and I was called to "come" every thirty-five seconds or so. Jeepers creepers, I'm three years old. How can I catch birds with all that going on?

Next, we both had to go to the vet and get a fat needle stuck in our necks to inject a rice kernel–sized microchip under our skin. Mine bled a tiny bit, but I got little sympathy. Now, if I get lost, I can be scanned by a vet or the animal rescue folks, and an agency called Home Again will be called with my chip number. Home Again will then call Jeanne and she will be exceed-ingly happy. Me too.

That's not all. We each got an electronic collar. And these, mind you, counted as part of our Christmas presents even though we had not request-ed them from Santa. I dance with excitement when Jeanne puts on my new e-collar because I know it means we're going outside—if not to the beach, somewhere else where there are birds, squirrels, people, and dogs. Don't get me wrong, I love my house, but "out" is better than just about anything else.

We also got new regular collars because our old ones were looking ratty. Jeanne switches our collars often because they get wet at the beach and have to be removed to dry in the laundry room where we change to dry ones. This is annoying because Jeanne has to reattach the rabies tags, Home Again tags, glow lights, therapy dog IDs, and "call my Mum" tags to two backup collars every day.

So today we bought these terrific little spring-snap, stainless steel carabiners. All my tags are now attached to a carabiner which simply clicks off the wet collar and onto the dry collar in a jiffy. Same for Bode. This keeps us safe and Jeanne relatively sane. Life is good.

Love,

Lady

Resolutions

Dear Diary,

What are New Year's resolutions? I had never heard of them until Bode and I got an assignment to come up with a couple of things we'd like to make better about ourselves during the coming year. Since it's mid-January, I thought this would be a good time to evaluate the pack's resolutions and our progress to date.

Bode (with Jeanne's encouragement) resolved to be less of a beggar for treats. I'll have to give him a D-minus so far. The boy has no shame and will hone in on any man, woman, or child who might have a morsel in a pocket. He'll even eat the pocket lint if it smells like the morsel. You'd think it was filet mignon. He's got eleven months to get his act together.

I thought I might resolve to run faster so as to be able to *catch* the birds at the beach, but Jeanne said that isn't a kosher resolution. She advised that, instead, I might consider chasing fewer squirrels around the yard. I would (generously) give myself a D-plus on this daunting challenge. Well, it's only January. There's still time.

Jeanne made a resolution I didn't understand. She wants to find things to be happy about every day. Hey, I wake up and go to sleep happy every day. What's the big deal?

She said Bode and I remind her about living in the moment and enjoying life's simple pleasures. That makes her resolution so much easier. (Like, since we're doing all the work, isn't that cheating?) For example, she wakes up in the dark of the night and watches Bode and me splayed out on the bed with our sides rising and falling at each secure breath. She says it brings her peace and joy.

Watching me snuggle up to a second grader as he reads with one hand stroking my head and the other holding the book makes her boundlessly happy. And when the disabled folks we visit smile as we lick their faces or hug them, Jeanne absolutely glows. Bode and I do too.

Love,

Lady

Snuggling up to second-grade readers is Lady's specialty.

Winning Jonathan Over

Dear Diary,

This morning we made our weekly trip to hear the second graders read. Besides the beach, this is my favorite place to visit.

Up to today, everyone in Miss Cahill's class had read to me, except for Jonathan. Now it was his turn.

I sat patiently on the purple Pilates mat and waited for him to select just the right book. It took him a little longer than his classmates usually take, so while waiting I enjoyed looking around at the other kids. They were supposed to be ignoring me, but of course they couldn't resist secretly waving their hands at me underneath their tables. My tail slapped the floor happily in response.

Jonathan approached my mat but chose to sit several feet away on the alphabet rug. When we invited him onto the mat, he said, "I'm afraid of large dogs." Did he mean me? Jeanne was quick to assure him that we understood. Looking quite serious, Jonathan replied, "But I *really* want to read to Lady." Wow. My heart skipped a beat when I heard this. Seven years old and maybe forty-five pounds on his slender frame. Brave as a soldier. Facing my sixty-five pounds of flyaway hair, he opened the book. After running his fingers through his spikey jet-black hair, and pushing up the wire-framed glasses that dominated his little face, he began to read chapter 1 in a soft, strong voice.

I tuned one ear to the part about animals in the snow, and with the other I listened to my instincts saying, "Baby steps, baby steps." I edged toward Jonathan. He kept reading. A page or two later, I edged still closer.

When I quietly snuggled next to his leg, a tiny smile lingered at the corner of his mouth.

Midchapter, I stuck my head in the middle of the open book on Jonathan's lap. Without missing a beat, he pointed to a girl dog on the page whose hair was the same color as mine. I moved my head away so he could continue reading, but I left my paw on his leg.

I was sorry when the chapter was finished. Jonathan stood up and let me shake hands with him. Then he bent over, closed his eyes, and rested his cheek on the top of my head. "Bye, Lady," he said. I think I'm in love.

Love,

Lady

Fund-raising Dinner Debut

Never in her wildest dreams did Lady expect to have fans.

Dear Diary,

    This past weekend, I was thrilled to attend a spaghetti dinner fund-raising event in North Myrtle Beach. When the invitation arrived, I felt like a debutante about to go to her first ball. As I sent back our RSVP (that's French for "heck yah"), I admit that I did suffer some momentary reservations and insecurities. What would I wear? Who would I sit with? Would I be able to lie down? What if I got nervous and "had to go"?

    The attire issue was swiftly resolved when Jeanne pulled out my spiffy new aqua and black therapy dog kerchief. This, together with a sleek black collar, and voila! (That's French for "get a load of *that*.") Naturally, we scheduled a pre-dinner beauty parlor session so I would look and smell my best. Party down!

    I had never seen several hundred humans in one room before, so it promised to be a terrific people-watching night. I decided to sit with my beach-walking buds and close to many of my peers on our therapy dog team. I love the camaraderie we share while working together.

The super-sized service dog pack was in our vicinity, parked in an orderly fashion on a large mat. Politely, we exchanged friendly glances. I noticed that when people held out money, these pups would take it in their mouths and drop it in a large donations jar. I thought it would be neat to take a few bucks *out* of the jar so I could buy a package of Pup-Peroni the next time we're in Walmart. I got THE LOOK.

I soon realized that I shouldn't have been worried or nervous about this dinner because all the two-legged guests were extremely kind and friendly. Aren't dog people the best? They approached me gently, introduced themselves, and told me they knew who I was from reading my *Lady Grams*. One lady said she would get up in the morning, make her coffee, and then immediately pull up my daily *Lady Gram*. Eventually, she started to postpone her morning coffee to go straight to her computer and read about my latest adventure. Compliments like that make my heart swell up.

I'm constantly amazed at the opportunities I've had since being rescued from my chain-link pen eight months ago. I've met people, learned things, and seen places that had previously existed only in my wildest dreams.

Many of you have so generously given your time, talent, and money to benefit dog causes. As one of your most grateful beneficiaries, I say simply and sincerely, "Merci."

Love,

Lady

Called off the Bench

Dear Diary,

Sometimes I feel like the scrawny kid on the football team relegated to warming the bench who never seems to get called out on the field to play. I'm frequently stuck in Lulu's back seat while Bode is chosen to jump out and strut his stuff. I hang my head out the open car window, thinking, *Pick me, coach; pick me!* But when that rear hatch lifts, it's only Bode who is asked to perform.

Most often, this happens after I've heard friends confide to Jeanne that their dogs love people but are aggressive toward other dogs. So we try to help them. Usually it turns out that these dogs are not vicious, just ill at ease and inexperienced at tolerating their canine peers. I remember being like that when I first joined this pack. I even wrote about it in several earlier *Lady Grams*.

Since then, I've been taught that exposure to a dog who exudes calm energy can be extremely valuable to a dog and owner who need help "playing nice" with others. It's sort of like those post ponies that escort the thoroughbreds to the starting gate at the Kentucky Derby. Having a good role model is one of the best training tools.

So once we've seen that an allegedly dog-aggressive dog knows basic obedience and can be controlled on leash by its handler, Jeanne will trot out Bode to meet the wayward student.

Though it ticks me off a tad that *he's* always chosen for the job, I must admit that Bode truly is Mr. Laid-Back, a.k.a. the King of Calm Energy. Me? I'm the Queen of High Energy, the exuberant kind rather than the calm.

Over the past few months, though, I really have shown that I can switch gears from excited to calm when necessary, for example when nestled against the leg of a second grader who's reading to me, or when saying hello to one of the older folks we visit.

A couple of weeks ago, Bode and I remained in the car while Jeanne was greeting Roxie, a nice-looking mixer girl, possibly part shepherd, corgi, and yellow lab. Roxie is around my age. She and Jeanne got to know each other through a few training visits. We were returning this week to help her learn to tolerate other dogs.

So I sat glumly by the car window as Jeanne walked to the back, where Bode was primed to jump out. Well, imagine my surprise when the back hatch opened and *I* was called onto the field! Yippee! The leash was clicked onto my collar, and I hopped out to meet Roxie, nose to bum. We sniffed appreciatively, tails wagging, all happy ears and hackles.

Then we walked. (I guess I could be accused of strutting, so pleased was I to be the chosen training associate.) We went about half a mile without so much as an incident. I became queen of the four Cs: calm, cool, collected, and confident. Roxie followed my example. It was way fun. When I can help another dog overcome some of the same issues I faced only a year ago, I know I've "come a long way, baby."

I admit to having had a slight smirk on my cute copper-colored face when we returned to Lulu, where this time it was Bode's head sticking out the window, waiting patiently.

Love,

Lady

The Fine Art of Fetching

Dear Diary,

How good a fetcher am I?

If it weighs less than five pounds, I probably have fetched it. I *love* fetching. I haven't mastered all the nuances yet, such as waiting to be asked to fetch something, or immediately delivering the fetched item.

I like to wiggle and prance in circles, fiercely shaking the fetched item in my mouth, all the while staying about six inches out of Jeanne's grasp. To me, this is not about teasing. It's the fine art of fetching.

Here are some of my favorite fetching targets:

- Plastic Bottles – A canine ear cleanser bottle with the cap removed so as to leave a trail of liquid while carrying it around the house.
- Clean Clothes – Any article of clothing dropped during dryer unloading with socks as a particular favorite.
- Neighbors' Belongings – Rayne's toys from the yard next door, especially her pink Dora umbrella and her bottles of bubble-blowing liquid. Catcher's toys are fun too, her rubber balls being a prize acquisition. If only they were the self-throwing variety.
- Sunglasses – Sunglasses from the Subaru dashboard fetched as soon as Jeanne exits the car, usually returned with one lens missing.
- Cell Phone – Last time I nabbed it, the dang thing slipped out of its case while I was dancing around. While I did return the case fairly promptly, the phone remained on the closet floor where it lay missing for hours. That qualified me for THE LOOK.

- Brushes and Cotton Balls – Grooming brushes and cotton balls from our beauty parlor box while Jeanne is trying to spiff us up for a therapy dog visit. Cotton balls are usually swallowed, not returned—at least, not until about twelve hours later.
- Shoes – Shoes galore. Slip them off while watching TV or on computer, and I'm on it in a flash. The master bedroom closet is a favored hunting ground. Yesterday I returned one new stiletto. (So it was two inches shorter than when I fetched it. She shouldn't be trying to walk in those things anyhow.)
- Dirty Laundry – Hamper items, with a special fondness for underwear. I like to leave them on the living room floor to be discovered when company walks into the room.
- Bedding – Pillows can be enjoyable, but nothing beats the comforter off the king-size bed. The main challenge is not tripping on it while dragging that puffy monster from room to room. One time I made it as far as the kitchen. It's the best kind of fun because when Jeanne turns around and sees me with my "kill," all she can do is laugh. I love to make her laugh. After all, I'm a therapy dog!

Love,

Lady

"Look at what I brought you."

Comparing Company and Fish

Dear Diary,

Some people say that company is like fish—after three days they both begin to smell. My company has been here for ten days, and they still smell terrific. I check them hourly, if not more often.

Fifi and Fluffy (yup) are seven-year-old Lhasa apso sisters, and Cosette is an eight-month-old cockapoo and veteran therapy dog. They're staying at my house while their parents are on a cruise.

I secretly refer to Cosette as Shadow, because she spends all her waking hours within a foot of Jeanne's right ankle. She follows her everywhere. I used to be like that, so I know how she feels.

The Lhasa pups like to lounge on the red love seats in the living room on which, might I interject, Bode and I are not allowed to sit. Okay, maybe a tad of jealousy has reared its ugly head. While I'm at it, I'll tell you a few other issues I have with our company.

Foremost, they eat ever so slowly, grazing nonchalantly while, if I even look in their direction, I'm required to "leave it" until hell freezes over. Doesn't matter if they are served beef, chicken, or kibble—they peck like little hens, strolling back and forth in front of their dishes. Since by then I've already literally inhaled my own food, I just watch. And wait. And drool.

Speaking of hens, my bedroom has turned into a girls' dorm. The guest pups don't seem to know that Bode is a boy, and I sure won't tell. They make me laugh when Jeanne announces at bedtime, "Little ones, kennel!" They hop off the king-size bed and trot efficiently into their respective crates. It's way cool. Plus, that leaves lots more room for Bode and me to stretch out on the big bed.

I have to admit that they are cute as all get out, even though they do steal some attention away from me. I like having the company. They're much more adorable than fish.

Love,
Lady

Honored for Volunteer Work

.

Dear Diary,

I'm proud to report that this week I was honored at a sit-down brunch at Union Elementary School, along with about eighty two-legged volunteers. Union is where I go every week to snuggle up to the second graders while they read to me.

As usual for public appearances, I had my nails trimmed, teeth brushed, ears cleaned, and coat groomed. Dressed in my pink bandanna, I was party ready.

I clearly haven't been to charm school, so when a cute little third-grade hostess politely pulled back a chair from our table, I thought she meant it was for me. Quick as a bunny, I hopped right up onto that little chair with the idea of continuing onto the tabletop. Simultaneous gasps of shock from Jeanne and Ronna nixed that notion in no time flat! Somewhat embarrassed, I retreated and joined Bode on the purple Pilates mat on the floor.

To open the event, we all stood up and sang the National Anthem. Given some of the tough notes to reach in that song, at one point I was forced to stifle an inappropriate howl. Then the fifth graders sang for us, ending with a terrific jazz number. They put on sunglasses and snapped their fingers, which got me all jazzed up.

A contingent of kindergartners followed, assigned to reciting a group poem about volunteers. As their line passed Bode and me while filing into the room, many dead serious little faces lit up with mischievous delight. I'm glad that seeing us helped ease some of their apprehension about performing.

Everyone's placemat was an original work of art drawn by a first grader, and we were encouraged to take them home. Jeanne's says, "Thanks for making Union shine!" and it's now hanging on the fridge.

The main course was quiche. Luckily, I don't like it, but the aroma momentarily captured Bode's interest. He got THE LOOK and sat back down. Fresh fruit together with jalapeno home fries didn't appeal to me either, but the two-legged diners tucked right into theirs. I noticed several volunteers smiling behind their napkins as a young server stopped to pat me and then continued on to deliver a plate of food. Some things are more important than hygiene.

After brunch came some speeches. Lots of people expressed appreciation, which prompted a great deal of enthusiastic applause. It made me feel proud that I'm able to help children read. I love applause. Afterward, lots of students came over to greet us, just like old friends.

As the morning's activities concluded, all the volunteers posed for a group photo. Bode and I were asked to sit front and center. This made everyone smile nice for the picture. You know me, always on the (therapy dog) job.

Love,

Lady

Putting On the Dog

Lady dons a chic bandanna for her first gala.

Dear Diary,

Another first for the rescued girl! Last night we found ourselves in a gigantic ballroom, elegantly decorated in a Kentucky Derby theme. I was entranced. We were there to attend the North Myrtle Beach Chamber of Commerce 2012 Annual Awards Gala, for which Canine Angels was a nominee. There were hundreds of people and a wonderful band playing dance music. I'm just learning to dance, but so far we haven't progressed past the living room.

Beautiful ladies were attired in fine dresses and exotic hats. Men sported natty tuxedos. All decked out in my pink Dollar Store bandanna, I fitted right in. *Trés chic.* (That's French for drop-dead gorgeous.) I am *so* moving up in this world.

Plumed hats served as centerpieces on tables laden with linen napkins, shiny glassware, finely-printed menus, and programs detailing this lavish event. Eight pieces of silverware adorned each place setting. The previous record for silverware at any event I have attended was five. Not that I am allowed to use any of them, but for a girl whose daily place setting consists of a pink plastic bowl, it was impressive.

I happily settled down under Jeanne's chair, next to Larry McMahan and his service dog, Abby, a former houseguest of ours. I didn't have much interest in the menu until the filet mignon was served. That quickly got Abby's and my attention. If I might offer a tiny complaint about the rules of this pack, it would be that food from the table to my lips is absolutely taboo.

But Larry has no such rules in his pack. Better still was the coincidence that my new friend, Kathy, sitting on our other side, does not eat red meat. So when Jeanne excused herself from the table, Abby and I were quick to surrender to divine providence. I have no idea whether our friend, King, who was sitting several seats away, was equally lucky. When it comes to filet mignon, it's every dog for herself.

The awards were announced after dinner. Although Canine Angels made it as far as national-level consideration, we were not selected as Nonprofit of the Year—this time. However, just being considered is quite an honor, especially for a fledgling organization scarcely more than a year into nonprofit status. Our congratulations go to the winners.

I heard everyone talking about the hundreds of letters of support that helped secure our nomination for Nonprofit of the Year. How fortunate we are to have so many fans, supporters, and volunteers. Thank you, wonderful people.

Love,

Lady

The Tables Have Turned

Dear Diary,

I remember having previously written about the first time I went to a dinner party, golf tournament, awards luncheon, fund-raiser, or other event that a dog, especially one rescued from a chain-link pen, might not normally be permitted to attend. Each time that special pink bandanna came out of the drawer, I knew we were stepping out. Back in those days I'd sometimes be so nervous that I would stick my head in the corner, making it difficult to get that scarf on.

But I managed to survive those occasions; in fact, I soon learned to bask in the limelight of all the attention and affection people poured out to me. Bode's laid-back example was a huge help toward calming my fears. Now I shimmy with glee when the pink bandanna is tied around my neck.

I'm proud to report that I've become something of a voice of experience, so I'm often called upon to assist fellow canines who need to learn the ropes of public appearances. This week I was delighted to help Justice, a handsome brindled pit bull who's a part-time addition to our therapy dog team.

Justice accompanied Bode and me to a fund-raiser on the waterfront deck at the Patios Restaurant in Little River. There were people everywhere. Service dogs, too. A pretty vocalist was singing sixties songs. The big deck was ringing with the loud sounds of laughter, eating, drinking, socializing, and sales of raffle tickets. King and Leroy were busy taking cash donations in their teeth and dropping them into a bucket. It was a happy, happening place.

From the moment Lulu's back hatch opened, I caught the scent of uncertainty coming from Justice. Sure—he hopped out willingly and moved off with a purposeful stride, head held high. But his eyes had that blank deer-in-the-headlights look as he took in the scene and hustled into formation, safely positioning himself between us two goldens. This was his first big social event.

As soon as the purple Pilates mat hit the floor beside our chosen table, we three were on it, well situated to catch our breath and get the lay of the land. My general preference is to squirm under Jeanne's chair. Bode tends to hang out under the table, where an unsuspecting soul might accidentally drop a crumb of dinner. Justice sat stoically. That is, until he got THE LOOK and decided to lie down.

Then, miraculously, a man at an adjacent table did drop a piece of hot dog, which landed between his feet. Although still stunned by the sights and sounds, Justice saw it fall and looked at me for guidance. Bode was staring at it in a trance, as though it might levitate and disappear into thin air. I had just about made a decision to go for it when Jeanne swooped down with a napkin and scooped it up and into the trash. Curses—foiled again.

Justice gradually caught on to being petted, cooed to, complimented, scratched behind the ears, and all that other great stuff. He never really needed any guidance from Bode or me on that score. I give him an A for gaining brand-new social skills at a large and scary gathering.

Love,

Lady

Mother's Day Reverie

Dear Diary,

    I've had my share of mothers.

    In only three years, three seems like a lot.

    The first was my birth mother, who gave me life.

    Second was the mother who surrendered me to a cause she believed in.

    The third is Jeanne.

    Third time's a charm.

    Happy Mother's Day to Jeanne and all my surrogate mothers out there who have offered their love and support throughout my transition to life as a therapy dog.

    Love,

    Lady

Ain't Nuttin' but a Hound Dog

Dear Diary,

Yippee! We have company for three days. Scooter is a hunk of a Treeing Walker coonhound mixer. He's studying to be a therapy dog like me, so I'm trying to set a good example for him. He is just about my size, the picture of happiness, and loves to play! Since Scooter already has excellent manners, this visit is mostly about socialization, rest, and recreation.

We chase each other through the waves, race after birds to no avail, and generally roughhouse, jostling each other whenever we can. It's utterly joyful to experience and even more so to watch. Well, most of it is joy, except when lamps crash and stuff like that.

I love Bode with all my heart, but he is not fond of playing. He's more couch potato than fitness fanatic. If I try to engage him, he simply lies down and yawns. When Bode and I are home alone I'm reduced to throwing my ball against the fridge and catching it, while he snores away under the computer desk.

Scooter's problem at home is even worse. His indoor playmate is a cat named Cassie. Don't quote me, but I think that cat rules the roost. She tolerates no foolishness, as she calls it, from any dog, especially Scooter. Well, she is a *big* cat, some sort of coon variety from Maine.

So Scooter is as happy as I am to have a lively playmate for the weekend. Whenever I can't find him in the house, I know to check his big feather dog bed in the bedroom. Sometimes he sneaks off there for a bit of quiet time during a lull in the action. But he's always game to get up and take me on when I challenge him to a friendly joust.

This kind of company is serious fun! It's been three days and I haven't worn him out yet.

Love,

Lady

Notching a Library Card

Dear Diary,

I'm trying to type silently. Jeanne and Bode have headaches. Come to think of it, if they made dog aspirin, I'd be wolfing down a few myself. We just returned from our first visit to the local library's weekend reading program. Whew!

We practiced being read to on the purple mat this morning. I assumed when told "we're going to work" that we were headed for a visit with the second graders. Not. Twenty or so children—toddlers to ten-year-olds—were coming to meet us and hear a story at the library. Our job was to add to the fun of reading.

I've not encountered many toddlers, so I had to remember to be careful walking around tiny people no taller than my own height. They like to snuggle in, poke and prod a little, and thoroughly investigate you. When it stopped being fun, I quietly got up and sat behind Jeanne. Bode had some difficulties too. He licked one little guy on the face, who then told his mother, "The boy dog ate me." No serious repercussions, but I was glad it was the *boy* dog.

The preschoolers made us chuckle a lot, and we had to try hard not to laugh out loud until we got home. Here are some excerpts.

Six-year-old boy (to Jeanne): Are these your dogs?
Jeanne: Yes.

Six-year-old boy: Where's your husband?
Jeanne: Who else has a question?

Jeanne: What kind of pups would make good therapy dogs?
Five-year-old girl: White ones.

Jeanne: How should you act when you meet a new dog for the first time?
Five-year-old boy: I got new sneakers.

Then Jeanne told everyone about our beauty parlor regimen and how we prepare to make public visits:

Jeanne: How did *you* prepare for today's reading program visit?
Little kindergartner: I lost my front tooth.

Finally, one little guy raised his hand patiently, and Jeanne enthusiastically took his question. He said, "Lady is chewing your camera." Tattletale.

Love,

Lady

P.S. There was also a nice lady in a rocking chair reading about pirates, but I had my paws more than full with twenty kids.

Some Fans Weigh In

Dear Diary,

April 11th is the first anniversary of my rescue. Wow. What a year it has been. When I belly-crawled from my chain-link pen to Lulu that rainy Monday morning, I had a feeling my life was about to change. I had no idea how much. Chronologically, I am three years old, but I really began living only last year. I hope all the love and joy I've found during those twelve wonderful months has come alive for you on these pages, and that you have laughed and learned while reading my diary.

Love,

Lady

P.S. Several friends and family members honored me with personal messages on this occasion. I'm delighted to close by sharing some of their thoughts with you.

Dear Lady,

Your buoyant spirit has defied the laws of gravity. You have captured the hearts of nonbelievers and converted them into zealots for the cause of canine–human connection. You have given hope and purpose to every dog and every person who is now, or someday will be, involved in the Canine Angels effort. You have become a pinnacle of pride for us all and have made Jeanne, me, and everyone who has met you into better people. May you continue to be the inspiration you are to each and every Canine Angel and volunteer who follows.

Rick Kaplan

President, Canine Angels

To My Fair Lady,

The other day I recalled a family gathering we celebrated in April 2011. The exciting news we all shared with Jeanne was her anticipation of your arrival. She was so concerned that you might be overwhelmed by meeting a great many new people all at once that she decided to wait an extra week to bring you into the pack. It was nearly another four months before I got to meet you but, rest assured, through your colorful *Lady Grams* I always felt I was right there beside you. Sometimes I wondered if I could possibly ever master all the tasks you were asked to learn. Your successes, and those of your packmates, are well-deserved. You three ought to be proud of each other.

With lots of love,

Auntie J

Dear Lady,

It's been an amazing year for you. I know it took a lot of work and self-control for you to learn to be the "Lady" that you have become. I had high hopes when I was given the rare opportunity to sponsor you. You've exceeded my expectations by far. Every card and blog I get from you is a reminder of that. Thank you for all you are doing for others by sharing your kind heart. One day we'll finally meet, and I'll give you the hug you deserve!

Love,

JD

(USAF Major Joe Maxon)

Dear Lady,

I think you knew the day we picked you up that your life was just beginning. Not many people or animals have a second chance at making a life with purpose. It felt like you knew this was your chance, and you seemed willing to give it your best.

I love when you attack the morning beach walk ritual with wild abandon. After hours of training from Jeanne, you soon met other dogs on the beach with only mild interest and no aggression. Flying through the surf, you appeared to imitate the birds you chased. You pranced over the sand, beaming pure joy at everyone and everything around you.

You blossomed into an expert teacher's aide in the classroom. When second graders read, you now accept their affection readily. At first you were shy and a little unsure of what the children wanted. A fast learner, you soon understood that they want attention and acceptance, just like you.

You clearly took to therapy dog work happily and with determination. Congratulations to our girl!

Love,

Ronna

Hey Lady,

Has it really been only one short year since you entered our lives and our mah-jongg group? It seems like you've always been with us. At first you greeted us somewhat timidly. Now when we arrive you come running to the door to greet us with your tail wagging madly in an outpouring of affection.

You are also a great golf buddy who helps us keep our game in perspective. If we make a less-than-spectacular shot, you stay curled up in the golf cart. But, following an awesome chip shot, you're the first to jump out and come to the edge of the green to watch the putt holed. You are so much fun to be with!

You have brought comfort and joy to so many—from second graders to the aged. May you continue to enjoy the security and love you have found, and may we continue to write many more anniversary tributes to you.

With hugs and treats,

Jan